How To Build LEGO® Cars

**Written by
Hannah Dolan**

**Models by
Nate Dias**

CONTENTS

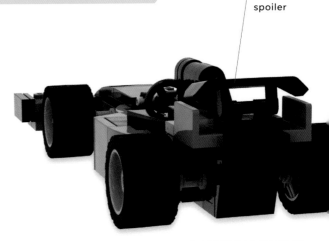

Wide rear spoiler

RACING CAR, PAGE 42

Large door opens from the top

DRIVERLESS CAR, PAGE 62

I hope you enjoy my designs!

MEET THE BUILDER

Nate Dias designed and created all of the cars in this book. He is a science teacher by day and a LEGO master builder by night! He won the first-ever series of the TV show LEGO® *MASTERS* in the UK.

When did you first start building? When I was five years old. I stopped building for a while at the age of 12, then started again at college thanks to one of my lecturers.

What's your favorite LEGO® piece? I love the 1x2 plate because it's the smallest element that you can use to build in more than one direction. For this book, my most useful piece was the 2x2x2/3 plate with two side studs. See if you can spot it!

Which car in this book would you most like to drive? The gingerbread car is fun, but I might be too tempted to eat it! It has to be the underwater car. I could show my son, Ned, some awesome sights.

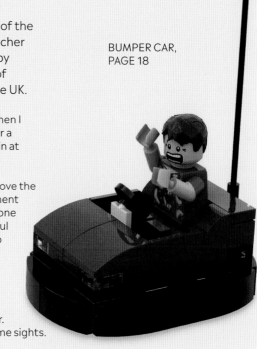

BUMPER CAR, PAGE 18

Opening rear door or "tailgate"

PICK-UP TRUCK, PAGE 50

HOW TO BEGIN

This book is all about building LEGO® cars, from their chassis to their bumpers to their roofs. Some are practical family cars, while others are speedy solo racers. There's an almighty monster truck, a space-ready moon buggy, a stretch limousine, and even a flying car. The cars start off easy and become harder as you move through the book, making it one imaginative building journey. Are you ready to begin?

BREAKING DOWN BUILDING

Each car is broken down into three to five important building stages. You might not have all the bricks you need, but you don't have to copy the models brick by brick. The breakdowns show techniques to inspire your own amazing ideas. There are also "ideas galleries" that focus on particular parts of cars, such as the chassis and engine, and ways to expand your builds.

The first picture is always the finished model

Each model is classed as easy, medium, or hard

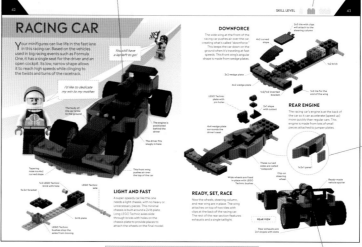

CAR MODEL

Some parts of models are broken down even more in these circles

The last step is one of the final stages or a rear view

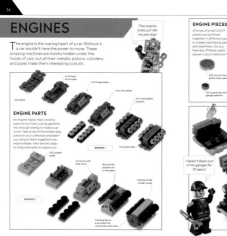

Smaller parts of car models or extra build ideas

IDEAS GALLERY

BRICK LISTS
If you'd like to see all of the bricks used in a particular car model, go to
www.dk.com/legocars

> *Always put the wheels on last so that your car doesn't roll away!*

TECHNICAL TIPS

These notes for builders will help you understand some of the LEGO words and terms that are used a lot in this book.

LEGO® DICTIONARY

2x3 brick

Studs are the round, raised bumps on top of bricks and plates. They fit into "tubes" on the bottom of pieces.

Bricks are found in most LEGO models. They are named according to how many studs they have on top.

1x2 brick

1x3 plate

Plates are similar to bricks because they have studs on top and tubes on the bottom, but they are much thinner.

Tiles are thin, like plates, but they have no studs on top.

2x2 tile

1x2 brick with LEGO® Technic hole

Holes inside bricks and other pieces can hold connectors such as pins, bars, and axles.

WAYS TO BUILD

Plates with clips attach to bars

Upward
The "easy" cars in this book mostly show pieces stacked on top of each other like this.

All around
Build moving parts or interesting shapes into your cars using hinged pieces or clips and bars.

1x1 brick with side stud

Thin plate holds the wheels

Sideways
More advanced models use a lot of pieces with studs on their sides for building sideways.

Downward
The wheels on cars are often attached underneath a car's body.

WAYS TO SCALE

Minifigure size
If you want minifigures to drive or ride in your car, think about how wide or tall your minifigures are and how much leg and headroom they will need inside.

Minus the minifigures
If you're happy to imagine your passengers inside, you could build cars of any size without leaving space for minifigures.

Microscale
Create a tiny traffic jam by building in microscale. Cars like this use small pieces in inventive ways.

OFF-ROADER

This classic off-road vehicle is a tough set of wheels, but it isn't tough to make. Built for adventure, it has four equally powerful wheels with heavy-tread tires that can navigate deep mud, steep hills, and uneven stud roads with ease.

1x4 tiles in a row create a smooth, boxy roof

Gray plates for the metallic front grille

Wheel with offset treads

See how to build this car's chassis on page 10

Buckle up, Rolo! This may be a rough ride.

I love a woof ride!

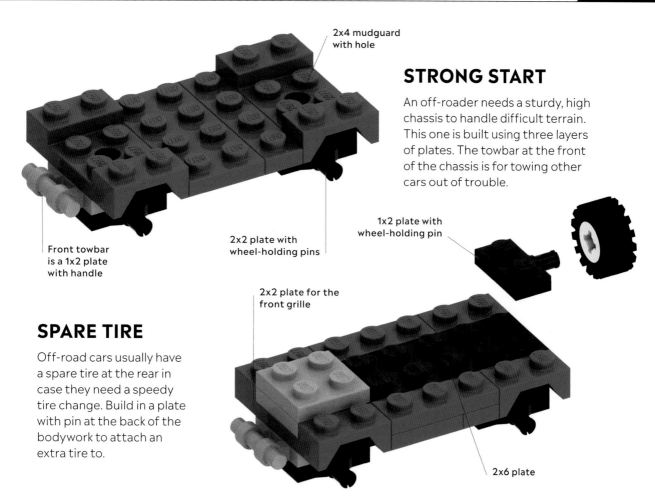

2x4 mudguard with hole

STRONG START

An off-roader needs a sturdy, high chassis to handle difficult terrain. This one is built using three layers of plates. The towbar at the front of the chassis is for towing other cars out of trouble.

Front towbar is a 1x2 plate with handle

2x2 plate with wheel-holding pins

1x2 plate with wheel-holding pin

2x2 plate for the front grille

SPARE TIRE

Off-road cars usually have a spare tire at the rear in case they need a speedy tire change. Build in a plate with pin at the back of the bodywork to attach an extra tire to.

2x6 plate

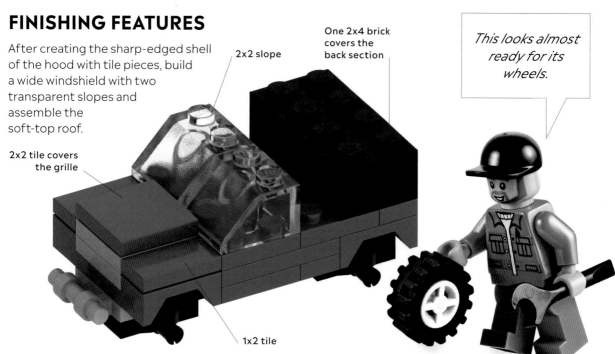

FINISHING FEATURES

After creating the sharp-edged shell of the hood with tile pieces, build a wide windshield with two transparent slopes and assemble the soft-top roof.

2x2 tile covers the grille

2x2 slope

One 2x4 brick covers the back section

This looks almost ready for its wheels.

1x2 tile

ROCKET CAR

This is a car that will never be caught in traffic. At the slightest sign of a jam, it can engage its rocket engines and propel itself through the skies and beyond. The rocket car's nose cone and small, curved wings or "fins" give it a pointed shape that allows it to blast off in seconds.

I've traveled through 20 galaxies, tracking you down. Now pay your library fine!

But my book isn't due back until Tuesday.

Lever pieces are joysticks for steering

Flaming rocket engine

Two 1x1 slopes make the windshield

Slope with slots forms the front of the fin

Nose cone is a 2x2x2 cone with an open stud

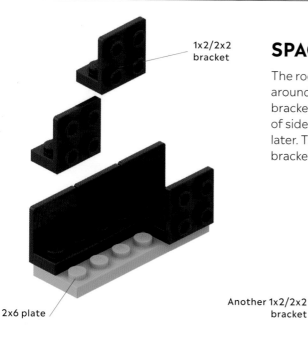

1x2/2x2 bracket

2x6 plate

SPACE BASE

The rocket car's narrow body is built around a 2x6 base plate. Six 1x2/2x2 bracket pieces fit onto it, creating lots of side studs to build out sideways from later. The space left in between the brackets is where the driver will sit.

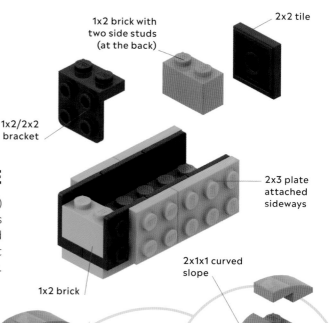

1x2 brick with two side studs (at the back)

2x2 tile

Another 1x2/2x2 bracket

2x3 plate attached sideways

NOT ROCKET SCIENCE

Sideways or SNOT (studs not on top) building might look complicated, but it's easy if you know which pieces to use. Add more useful SNOT pieces to build out sideways at the front and rear of the car.

1x2 brick

2x1x1 curved slope

2x1 inverted slope

1x2 tile with bar handle

This front bracket holds the nose cone

Side fins attach here

ALMOST FIN-ISHED

Now the rocket car is preparing to launch, with wheels and a windshield in place. Its smooth sides are also complete, with jumper plates where the side fins will go. The nose cone attaches sideways at the front, while the top fin fits onto a jumper plate's stud.

2x2 thin plate with wheel holder

Tiny pulley wheel piece

Skateboard wheels

CHASSIS

A chassis is the frame that supports the body of a vehicle, so it's the best place to begin any car model. There are a lot of ready-made LEGO® chassis frames to build your car designs around, but it's just as much fun to create your own.

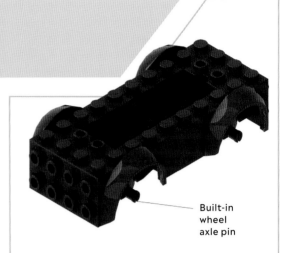

Built-in wheel axle pin

ALL-IN-ONE CHASSIS

This LEGO® Juniors chassis frame is a single piece. It has mudguards, wheel axle pins, and lots of side studs.

CHASSIS PIECE

This black cab uses a chassis piece with a recessed center. The stepped plates on its sides make it useful for building wider cars.

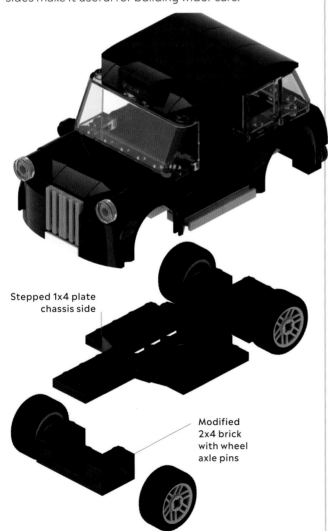

Stepped 1x4 plate chassis side

Modified 2x4 brick with wheel axle pins

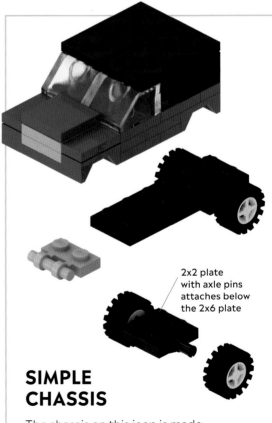

2x2 plate with axle pins attaches below the 2x6 plate

SIMPLE CHASSIS

The chassis on this jeep is made from just a few LEGO pieces—a narrow 2x6 plate and two smaller plates with axle pins for the wheels.

Can I take your taxi to the airport?

2x10 plate chassis

2x2 modified plate with wheel axles

LAYERED CHASSIS

This curvy vintage car is built around a single 2x10 plate with a 2x4 plate attached underneath to support its wider bodywork.

Great build! Now I'll tighten the wheel nuts.

WIDE CHASSIS

This chassis design is wide and low to the ground. The wheels are attached on the bottom layer, on either side of a square plate. There's a narrow 2x8 plate in the layer above, with smaller plates around it.

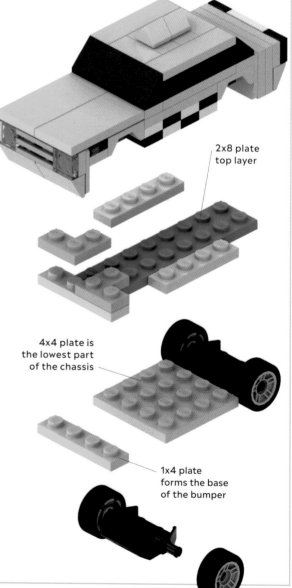

2x8 plate top layer

4x4 plate is the lowest part of the chassis

1x4 plate forms the base of the bumper

DRAGSTER

Start your engines.... This long, narrow car is designed to be first across the finish line on a drag racing circuit. It has a big engine and very light bodywork. A rear wing controls the amount of air or "drag" moving past it, allowing the dragster to reach incredibly fast speeds.

Find more racetrack building ideas on pages 88–89

A smooth 2x6 tile forms the top of the rear wing

Sometimes I drive it to the store to get milk.

1x2 tile with handle headrest

Pistol pieces are engine exhausts

Two 1x6 curved slopes create the front of the frame

Small, smooth tires at the front

LONG CHASSIS

A very fast car like the dragster needs a long and light chassis. This one is made from just one 2x16 plate. It can be seen from the outside of the car, so it's in a color that fits in with the color scheme. Two different plates with wheel-holding pins fit underneath the long plate.

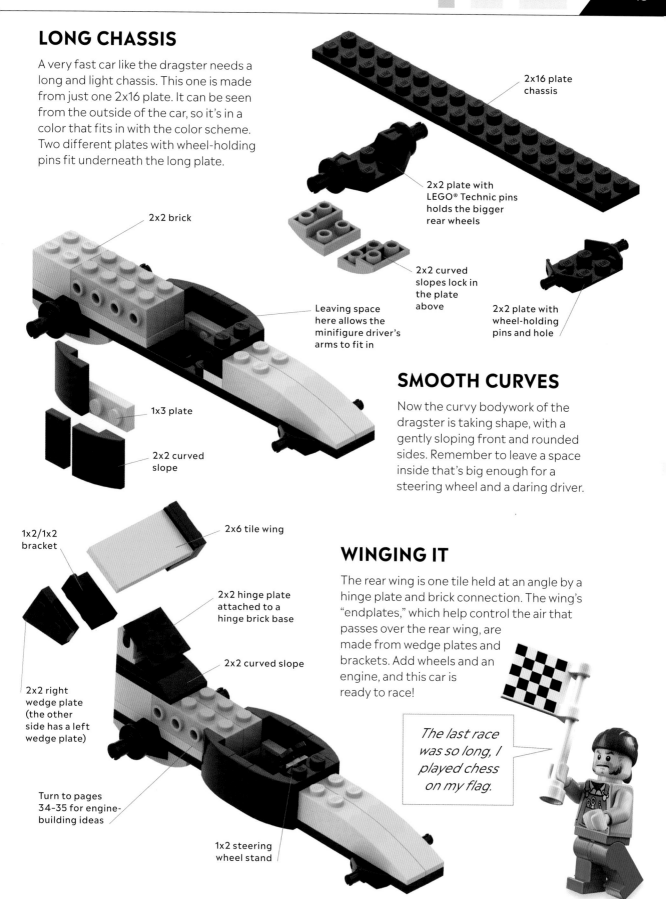

2x16 plate chassis

2x2 plate with LEGO® Technic pins holds the bigger rear wheels

2x2 brick

2x2 curved slopes lock in the plate above

Leaving space here allows the minifigure driver's arms to fit in

2x2 plate with wheel-holding pins and hole

1x3 plate

2x2 curved slope

SMOOTH CURVES

Now the curvy bodywork of the dragster is taking shape, with a gently sloping front and rounded sides. Remember to leave a space inside that's big enough for a steering wheel and a daring driver.

1x2/1x2 bracket

2x6 tile wing

2x2 hinge plate attached to a hinge brick base

2x2 curved slope

2x2 right wedge plate (the other side has a left wedge plate)

WINGING IT

The rear wing is one tile held at an angle by a hinge plate and brick connection. The wing's "endplates," which help control the air that passes over the rear wing, are made from wedge plates and brackets. Add wheels and an engine, and this car is ready to race!

The last race was so long, I played chess on my flag.

Turn to pages 34–35 for engine-building ideas

1x2 steering wheel stand

ANIMAL CARS

Turn your favorite furry or four-legged friends into the cutest cars! These animal automobiles all look very different, but they have the same basic chassis and bodywork design. Just build different faces and tail details at the front and rear to make all kinds of wildlife on wheels.

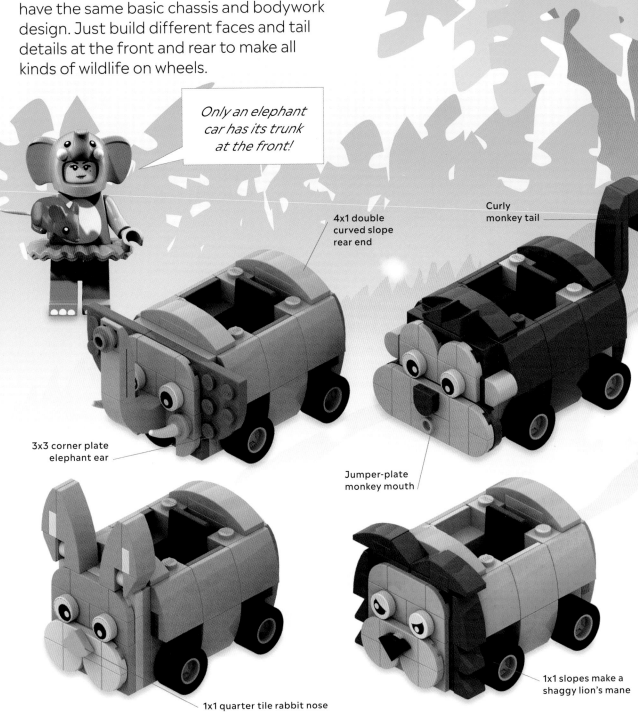

Only an elephant car has its trunk at the front!

4x1 double curved slope rear end

Curly monkey tail

3x3 corner plate elephant ear

Jumper-plate monkey mouth

1x1 quarter tile rabbit nose

1x1 slopes make a shaggy lion's mane

BASIC BODY

The animal cars' bodies are all made from the same pieces. Their small chassis are built around 2x6 plates with six more plates on top—two regular 2x2 plates and four 2x2 plates with wheel-holding pins.

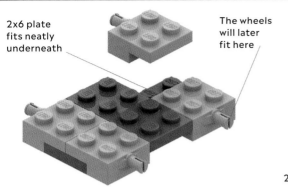

2x6 plate fits neatly underneath

The wheels will later fit here

SIDE STUDS

Now there are a lot of bricks on the plate chassis. Build in bricks with side studs on the front, back, and sides of the animal car body so that more pieces can be added sideways at the next stage.

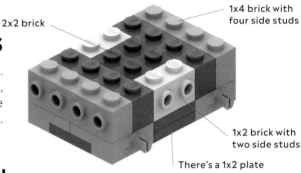

2x2 brick

1x4 brick with four side studs

1x2 brick with two side studs

There's a 1x2 plate here now, too

COZY CABIN

It's time to build the driver's cabin. The seat and steering wheel sit low within layers of plates, bricks, and panels.

4x1 double curved slope

1x2 steering wheel stand

2x2 driver's seat

1x2x1 panels create space for minifigure arms

Small wheels are now attached to the pins

MAKING FACES

Attach all kinds of animal features to the side studs on the bodywork. This elephant has big ears and a trumpeting trunk at the front, rounded sides, and a swishing tail at the back!

The back part is built around a 2x4 plate

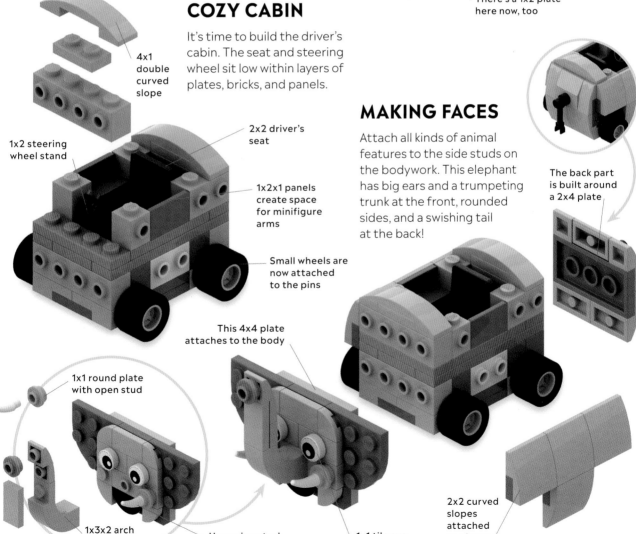

This 4x4 plate attaches to the body

1x1 round plate with open stud

1x3x2 arch brick trunk

Horn piece tusk

1x1 tile eye

2x2 curved slopes attached to plates

BUMPERS AND MIRRORS

Make your car models look more realistic by adding practical details to their exteriors. Build in mirrors so minifigure drivers can see the road around them and bumpers to protect your creations from bumps and collisions.

Large engine grille made from four vertical grille tiles

Two slopes with slots make a pointed grille

2x1x1 curved slopes form a wraparound bumper

BACK BUMPERS

Back bumpers often feature taillights, license plates, and trunk door handles. They can be curved or angular, detailed or simple. They can blend in with a car's body or stand out as points of interest.

These large, round tile headlight lenses stand out

VINTAGE CAR

Square 1x1 tail lights

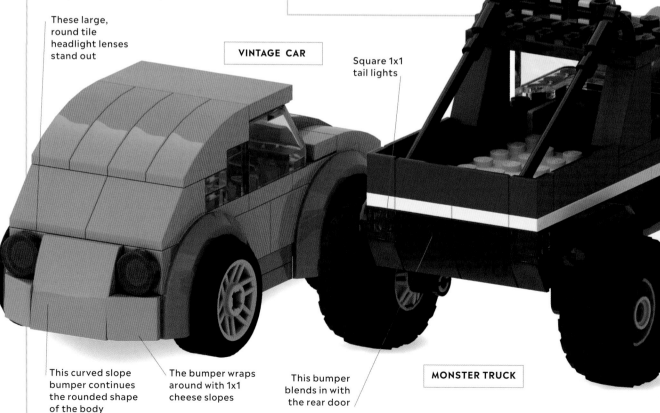

This curved slope bumper continues the rounded shape of the body

The bumper wraps around with 1x1 cheese slopes

This bumper blends in with the rear door

MONSTER TRUCK

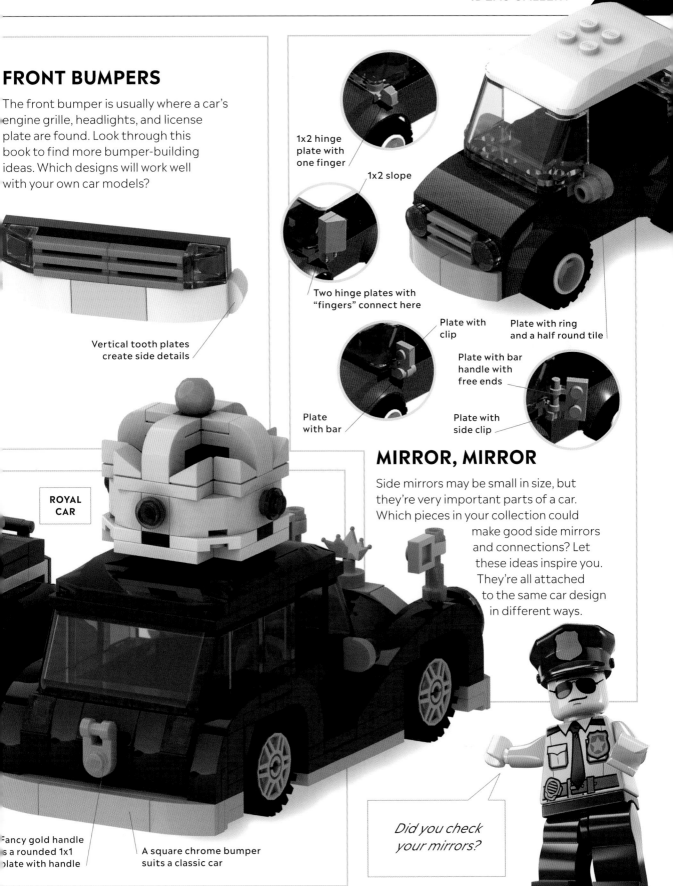

FRONT BUMPERS

The front bumper is usually where a car's engine grille, headlights, and license plate are found. Look through this book to find more bumper-building ideas. Which designs will work well with your own car models?

1x2 hinge plate with one finger

1x2 slope

Two hinge plates with "fingers" connect here

Plate with clip

Plate with ring and a half round tile

Plate with bar handle with free ends

Plate with bar

Plate with side clip

Vertical tooth plates create side details

ROYAL CAR

MIRROR, MIRROR

Side mirrors may be small in size, but they're very important parts of a car. Which pieces in your collection could make good side mirrors and connections? Let these ideas inspire you. They're all attached to the same car design in different ways.

Fancy gold handle is a rounded 1x1 plate with handle

A square chrome bumper suits a classic car

Did you check your mirrors?

BUMPER CAR

Your minifigures had better prepare for a bumpy ride in this carnival favorite. Small, electrically powered bumper cars have rubber bumpers around their bases so riders can race around and crash into each other, creating car-based chaos!

Electricity cable is an antenna piece

I haven't bumped you yet, darling.

Aaaaargh!

1x2 steering wheel stand and steering wheel

Transparent red 1x1 plate taillight

Build more than one bumper car for maximum chaos

Black tiles and curved bricks look like smooth rubber

All the fun of the fair!

FLAT BASE

This bumper car is built around a 4x6 base plate. Smaller plates build up the red bodywork and form the tiny head and taillights.

1x4 plate

This 1x2 brick with clip will hold the power cable later

Headlight is a transparent 1x1 plate

2x2 corner plate

REAR VIEW

1x1 plate

2x2 curved slope

1x2x1 panel

BUMPING SEAT

The next layer is the smooth surface of the bumper car's bodywork, made from curved slopes and bricks. Leave a space large enough for your minifigure to sit down inside the car.

1x1 brick with studs on two sides

Thin 2x2 plate with wheel holder

1x2 curved slope

BIG BUMPER

Turn over the car and build a wide bumper all around its edge. This bumper is made with small curved slopes, plates, and tiles. They attach to bricks with side studs on the underside of the 4x6 base plate. Add tiny wheels in the middle of the base to help your bumper car roll along.

UNDERSIDE VIEW

Skateboard wheels

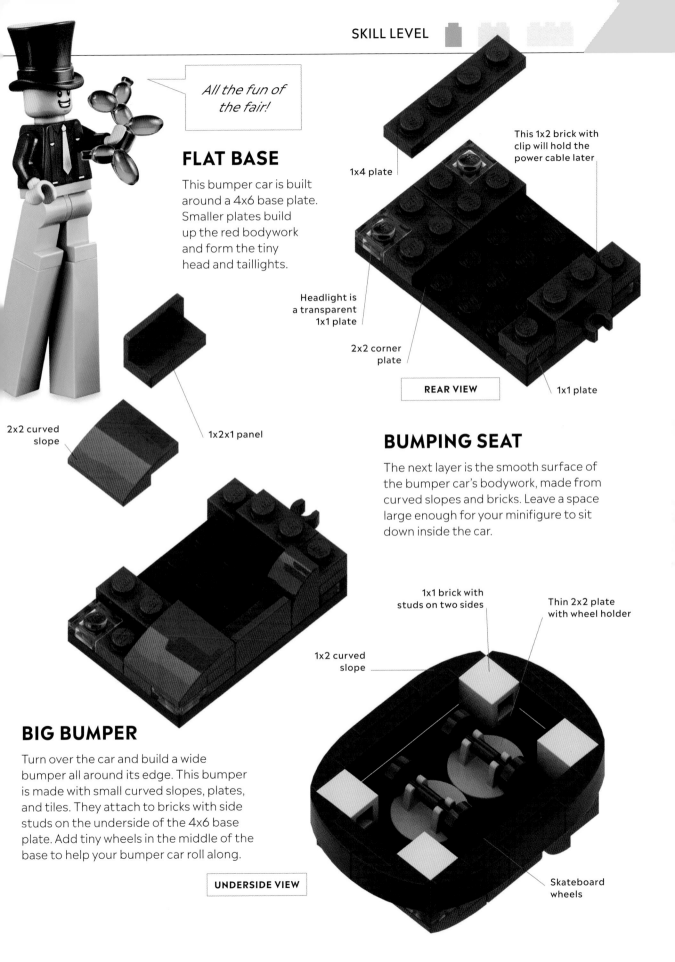

FAMILY CAR

A growing minifigure family needs a sizable car for getting around town and for carrying all the equipment that new babies need! This simple family car design has room inside for two minifigures. It's built around one large LEGO Juniors chassis piece, which has ready-made car doors and built-in wheel-holding pins.

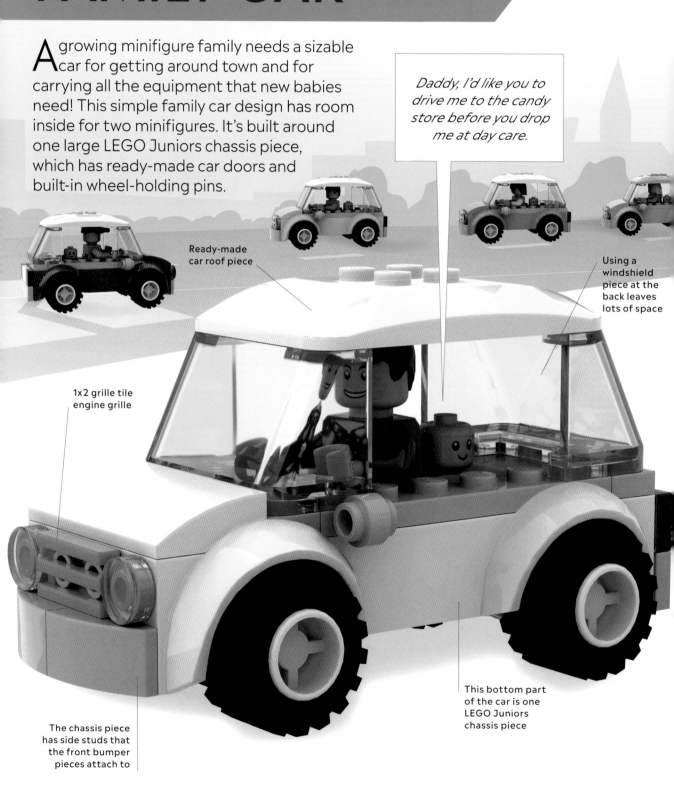

Daddy, I'd like you to drive me to the candy store before you drop me at day care.

Ready-made car roof piece

Using a windshield piece at the back leaves lots of space

1x2 grille tile engine grille

The chassis piece has side studs that the front bumper pieces attach to

This bottom part of the car is one LEGO Juniors chassis piece

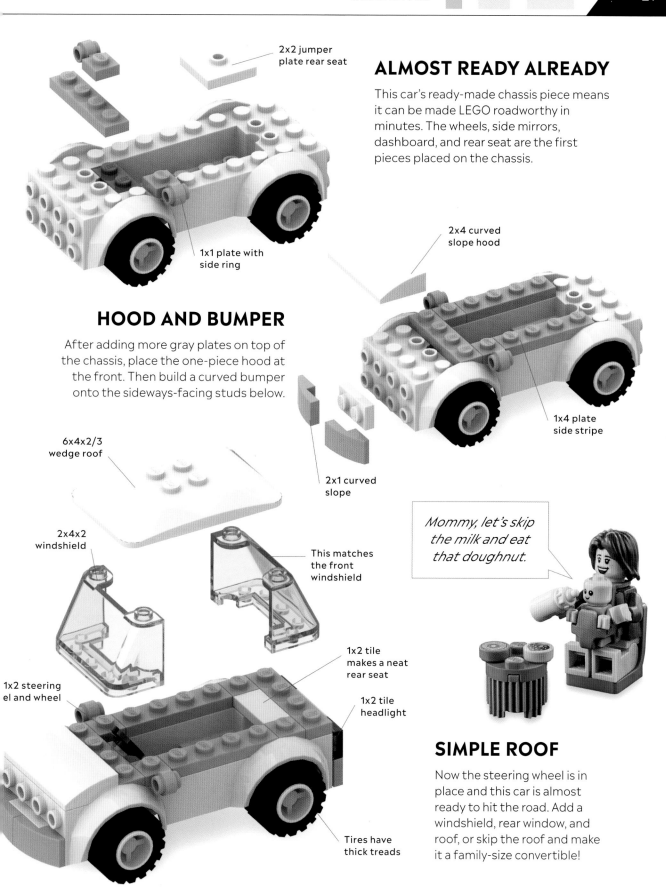

2x2 jumper
plate rear seat

ALMOST READY ALREADY

This car's ready-made chassis piece means
it can be made LEGO roadworthy in
minutes. The wheels, side mirrors,
dashboard, and rear seat are the first
pieces placed on the chassis.

1x1 plate with
side ring

2x4 curved
slope hood

HOOD AND BUMPER

After adding more gray plates on top of
the chassis, place the one-piece hood at
the front. Then build a curved bumper
onto the sideways-facing studs below.

1x4 plate
side stripe

6x4x2/3
wedge roof

2x1 curved
slope

2x4x2
windshield

This matches
the front
windshield

*Mommy, let's skip
the milk and eat
that doughnut.*

1x2 steering
el and wheel

1x2 tile
makes a neat
rear seat

1x2 tile
headlight

SIMPLE ROOF

Now the steering wheel is in
place and this car is almost
ready to hit the road. Add a
windshield, rear window, and
roof, or skip the roof and make
it a family-size convertible!

Tires have
thick treads

MINIFIGURE GEOMETRY

When building LEGO cars for minifigures, it's important to build the right amount of space inside to fit the dimensions of their bodies. They may also want a passenger to ride by their side, or they could need extra headroom to accommodate a hat or particularly voluminous hair!

Tiles leave lots of arm space

DRIVER ONLY = FOUR STUDS WIDE

Panel pieces give enough room

SEAT WIDTH

When sitting down, a minifigure's bottom half fits onto four studs—two studs at the front and two behind. But minifigures' arms are more than two studs wide, so build in open spaces around your car seats.

DRIVER AND PASSENGER = SEVEN STUDS WIDE

I'll need my arms free to lift the winner's trophy.

EXTRA ARM ROOM = EIGHT STUDS WIDE

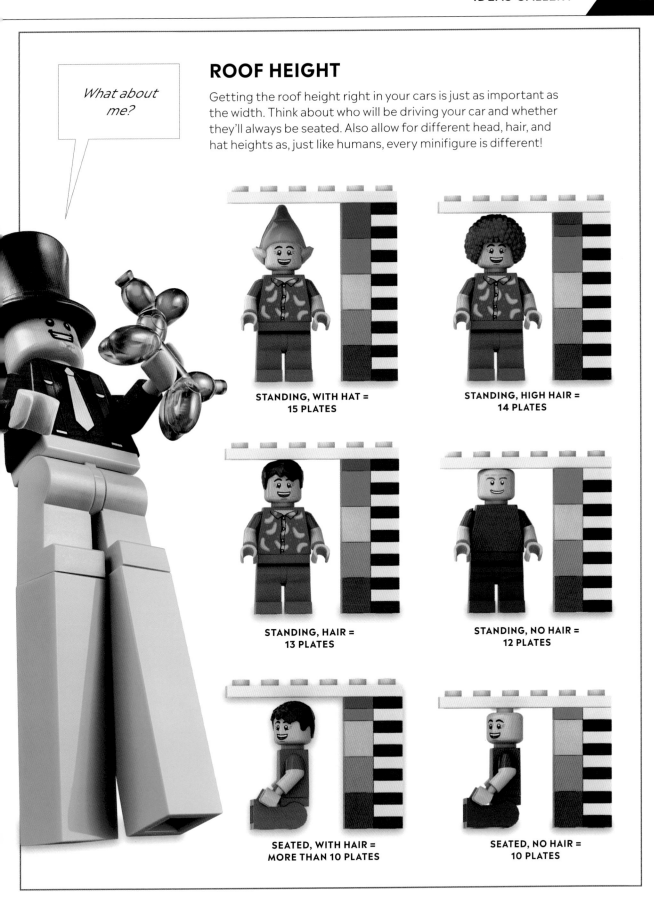

ROOF HEIGHT

Getting the roof height right in your cars is just as important as the width. Think about who will be driving your car and whether they'll always be seated. Also allow for different head, hair, and hat heights as, just like humans, every minifigure is different!

What about me?

**STANDING, WITH HAT =
15 PLATES**

**STANDING, HIGH HAIR =
14 PLATES**

**STANDING, HAIR =
13 PLATES**

**STANDING, NO HAIR =
12 PLATES**

**SEATED, WITH HAIR =
MORE THAN 10 PLATES**

**SEATED, NO HAIR =
10 PLATES**

AUTO RICKSHAW

Beep beep! Three-wheeled auto rickshaws can be found in many warm countries around the world, such as India. This one is small and speedy, so it can whizz along narrow city streets. Its open sides allow passengers to enjoy a cooling breeze as they ride along.

This is a window piece built into the canopy

1x4x2 windshield

Does it have room for my luggage?

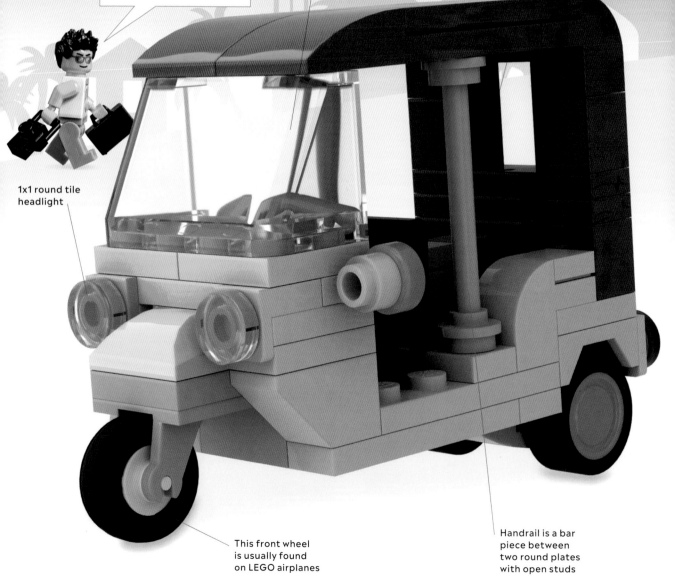

1x1 round tile headlight

This front wheel is usually found on LEGO airplanes

Handrail is a bar piece between two round plates with open studs

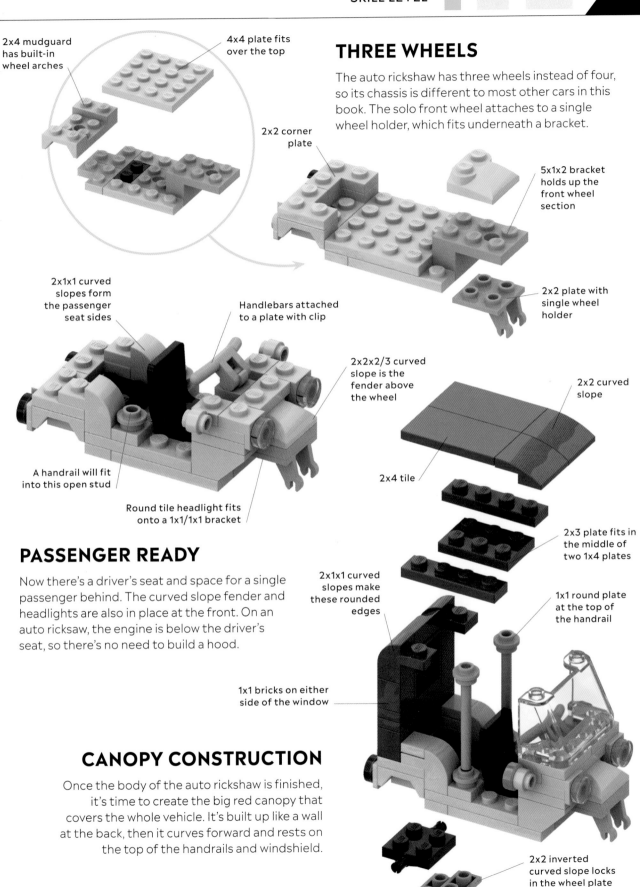

2x4 mudguard has built-in wheel arches

4x4 plate fits over the top

THREE WHEELS

The auto rickshaw has three wheels instead of four, so its chassis is different to most other cars in this book. The solo front wheel attaches to a single wheel holder, which fits underneath a bracket.

2x2 corner plate

5x1x2 bracket holds up the front wheel section

2x2 plate with single wheel holder

2x1x1 curved slopes form the passenger seat sides

Handlebars attached to a plate with clip

2x2x2/3 curved slope is the fender above the wheel

2x2 curved slope

2x4 tile

A handrail will fit into this open stud

Round tile headlight fits onto a 1x1/1x1 bracket

2x3 plate fits in the middle of two 1x4 plates

PASSENGER READY

Now there's a driver's seat and space for a single passenger behind. The curved slope fender and headlights are also in place at the front. On an auto ricksaw, the engine is below the driver's seat, so there's no need to build a hood.

2x1x1 curved slopes make these rounded edges

1x1 round plate at the top of the handrail

1x1 bricks on either side of the window

CANOPY CONSTRUCTION

Once the body of the auto rickshaw is finished, it's time to create the big red canopy that covers the whole vehicle. It's built up like a wall at the back, then it curves forward and rests on the top of the handrails and windshield.

2x2 inverted curved slope locks in the wheel plate

VINTAGE CAR

This boldly colored, compact classic car is a little piece of history. Designed in the style of practical family cars that were very popular from the 1960s, it has an iconic curved shape. It's perhaps even cooler today than it has ever been!

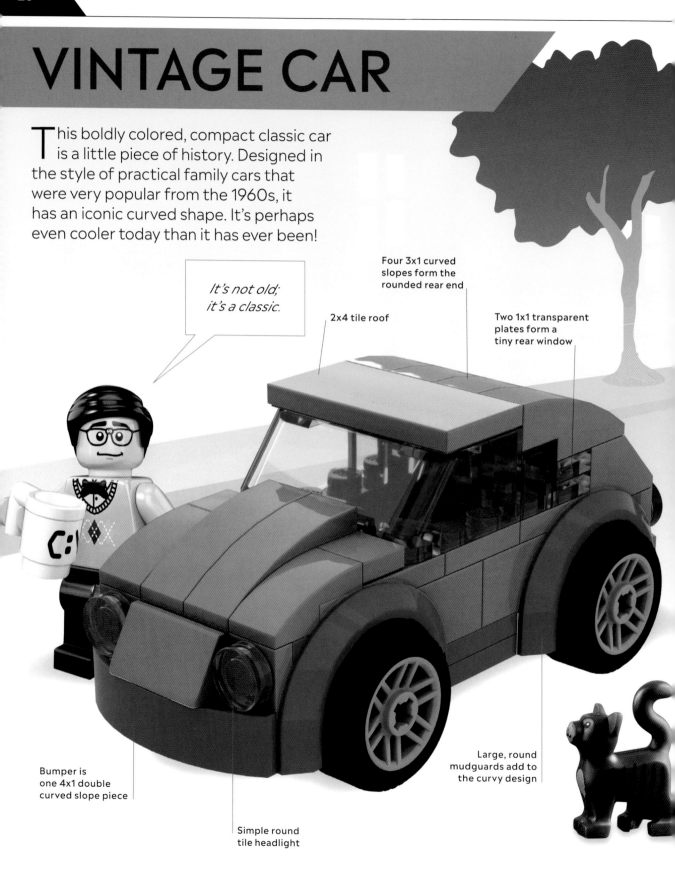

It's not old; it's a classic.

Four 3x1 curved slopes form the rounded rear end

2x4 tile roof

Two 1x1 transparent plates form a tiny rear window

Bumper is one 4x1 double curved slope piece

Simple round tile headlight

Large, round mudguards add to the curvy design

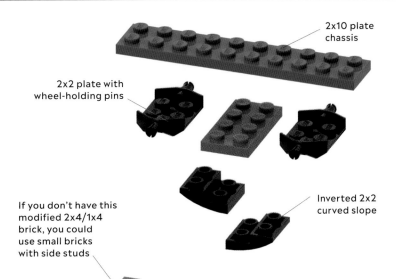

START THE CAR

The vintage car has a simple chassis of a 2x10 plate with wheel-holding plates attached underneath. A gray 2x4 plate also fits widthways under the chassis plate—this will form part of the car's gray "running boards" or trim.

2x10 plate chassis

2x2 plate with wheel-holding pins

Inverted 2x2 curved slope

If you don't have this modified 2x4/1x4 brick, you could use small bricks with side studs

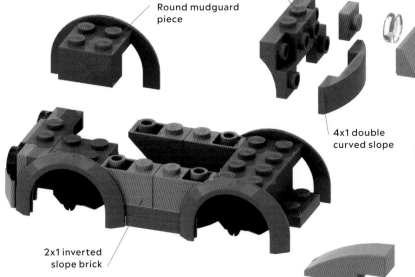

Round mudguard piece

1x2 slope

4x1 double curved slope

COMPACT CURVES

Now the vintage car has inverted slope side doors, which fit snugly behind the round arches of its mudguards. The lower sections of the front and rear bumpers add more curves to the vintage car's bodywork.

2x1 inverted slope brick

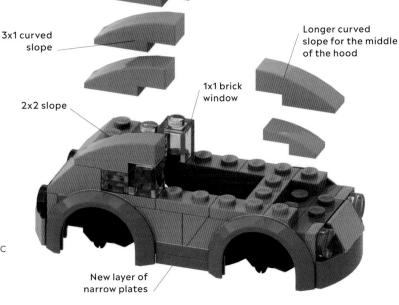

3x1 curved slope

Longer curved slope for the middle of the hood

1x1 brick window

2x2 slope

ROUND ROOF

The distinctive round shape of the vintage car's roof is mostly made from curved slopes in different sizes. Transparent blue plates and bricks then fit neatly into the small spaces underneath to form the rear windows. Add the hood and a roof tile on top, and this classic car has a new lease on life!

New layer of narrow plates

FUN FEATURES

For automobiles that are out of the ordinary, build in some funny or unusual features. Think about what your LEGO car will be used for, who will drive or ride in it, and what your minifigure passengers might need for comfort or to stand out on the road. Let your imagination take the wheel!

2x1x1 curved slope

This part of the crown is called the "monde"

2x2 macaroni bricks form the rounded sides

CROWN JEWELS

This car fit for a queen has a glistening gold crown on its roof, so there's no mistaking who's riding inside it. The crown has a base of white and black plates that look like a fur trim. Its distinctive golden arches are built from curved slopes and tiles. See more of the royal car on pages 86–87.

1x1 plate jewels attach sideways

2x2 wedge plate

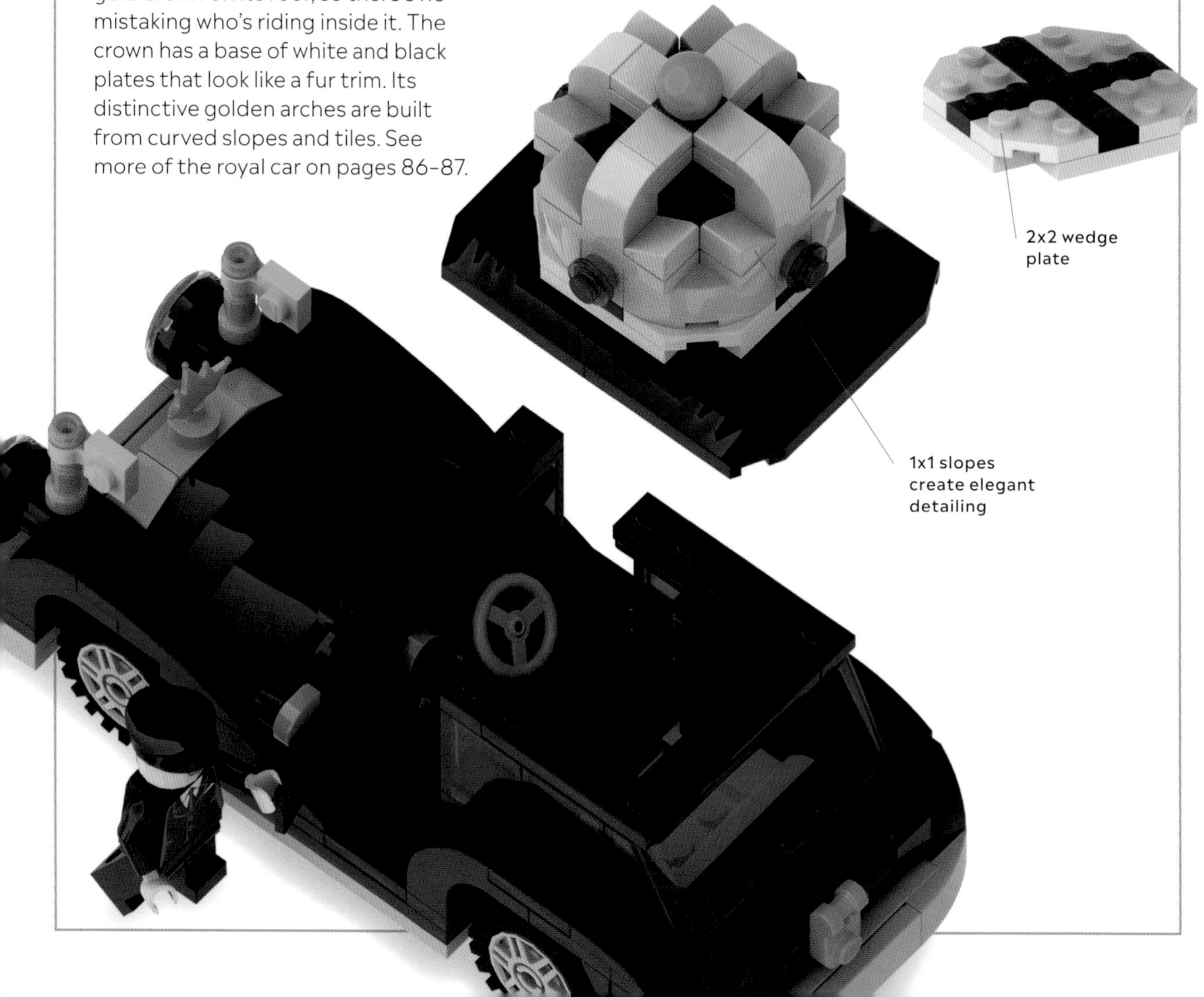

1x1 slopes create elegant detailing

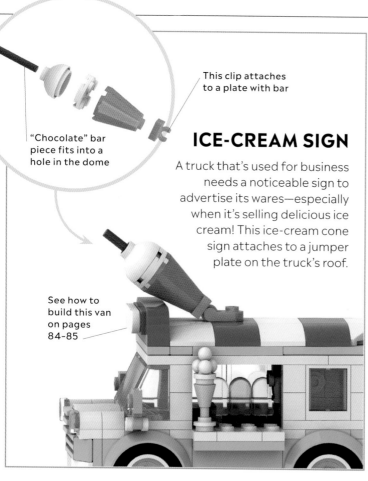

This clip attaches to a plate with bar

"Chocolate" bar piece fits into a hole in the dome

ICE-CREAM SIGN

A truck that's used for business needs a noticeable sign to advertise its wares—especially when it's selling delicious ice cream! This ice-cream cone sign attaches to a jumper plate on the truck's roof.

See how to build this van on pages 84-85

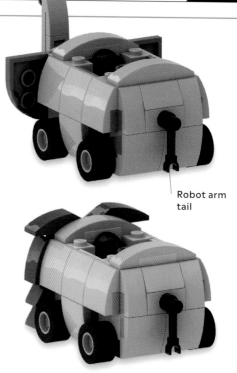

Robot arm tail

ANIMAL TAILS

The animal cars on pages 14–15 have adorable faces at the front, but they also have twisting, twirling, and twitching tails at the back! Each tail attaches to a side stud on the bumper.

Small plates form the beam

Inverted 2x1 curved slope

SAIL AWAY

You could build alternative parts of your car models to make them even more fun to play with. The pirate car on pages 72-73 has a skull sail—here's how it would look when it's "lowered."

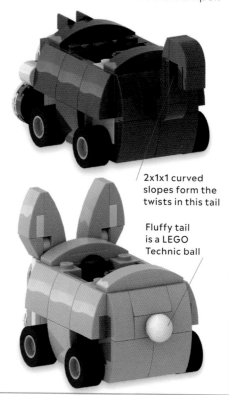

2x1x1 curved slopes form the twists in this tail

Fluffy tail is a LEGO Technic ball

CITY CAR

Not everyone needs spoilers and fancy features on their cars—sometimes less is more! This nippy, compact car has everything a busy city driver might need: a sturdy chassis, wide windows, and neat little wheels. As an added bonus, it will never struggle for a parking space!

Roof is one 4x4 tile with four studs on its edge

Windshield pieces form the front and back windows

We are both small and sophisticated.

4x1 double curved slope hood

Simple side stripe is a 1x3 plate

Smooth wheels for city roads

Me too!

SIMPLE BASE

The city car is built up from a ready-made vehicle base that has built-in wheel-holding pins and a 4x3 plate center section. If you don't have the piece, you could use regular plates instead.

2x2 plate

1x3 plate is the base of the car's side door

4x7x2/3 vehicle base

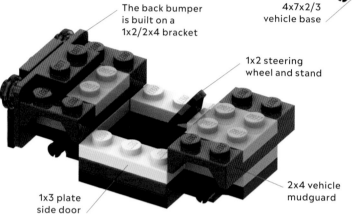

The back bumper is built on a 1x2/2x4 bracket

1x2 steering wheel and stand

1x3 plate side door

2x4 vehicle mudguard

SIDE STRIPE

Now the city car's side doors are taking shape. A white 1x3 plate adds a "go-faster" stripe to the door design. There are also tiny mudguards, a rear bumper, and a steering wheel.

BUMPER BRACKET

Like the rear bumper, the front bumper is built onto a bracket piece that has eight sideways-facing studs on it. The headlights, grille, and curved bumper all fit onto it.

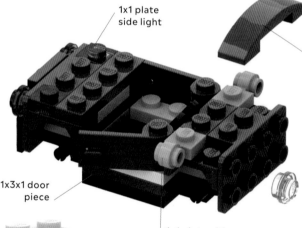

1x1 plate side light

This double curved slope is the hood

1x1 round plate headlight

This is a modified tile, but an ordinary one would work, too

1x3x1 door piece

1x1 plate with side ring is the side mirror

4x1 double curved slope splash shield

2x4x2 windshield

Jumper plate trunk door

WHEELY DONE

Add a windshield at the front and a matching piece at the back for the rear windows. A modified 4x4 tile for the roof tops off the build. Secure the small wheels on their wheel pins, then head off to explore the city!

Simple wheel trim

REAR VIEW

MOON BUGGY

Sam to Base ... Can you put my dinner in the oven?

2x2 inverted dish is a satellite dish

Drill piece in the tool storage area

A 1x1 round plate with bar holds this dish

Wide mudguards shield the driver from moon dust

This moon buggy is built to rove across the dusty, rocky surface of the moon so that astronauts can learn more about the landscape there. It has four heavy tires prevent it from floating away into space and two satellite-dish antennae for communicating with other astronauts or people back on Earth.

BUGGY BEGINNINGS

The moon buggy is built around just one 2x8 plate. Plates with wheel-holding pins attach underneath the plate, while 2x4 bricks and smaller bricks with side clips fit above it.

Tools will later attach to these 1x1 bricks with side clips

2x8 plate

2x4 brick

4x3x1 mudguard with curved arches

2x2 plate with wheel-holding pins

Large wheels will soon fit here

DUST GUARDS

The surface of the moon is covered with a thin layer of dust, so any moon buggy needs big mudguards around its wheels to protect its driver from sprays of dust. These mudguards fit onto the bricks above the chassis plate.

LUNAR EQUIPMENT

Now the moon buggy has steering and storage areas. Just before adding the wheels, build satellite dishes on the top so the buggy has all the equipment it needs for its moon missions.

Bar with mechanical claw

1x1 plate with bar fits onto a jumper plate's stud

1x2 slope dashboard

Antenna piece is the satellite dish pole

Wow, humans do exist!

2x2 curved slope makes a storage box lid

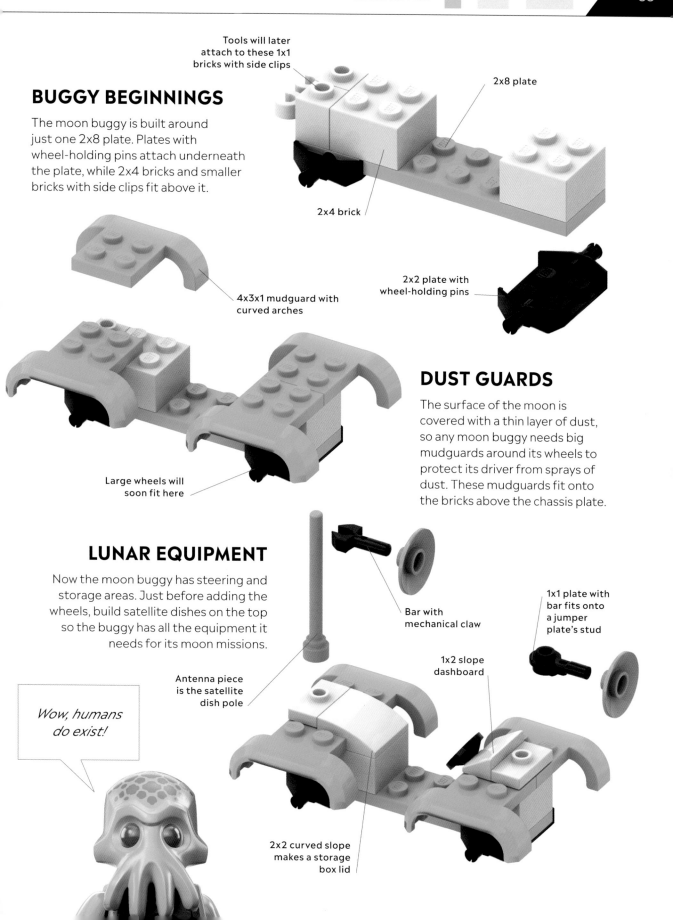

ENGINES

That engine looks just like my pet dog!

The engine is the roaring heart of a car. Without it, a car wouldn't have the power to move. These amazing machines are mostly hidden under the hoods of cars, but all their metallic pistons, cylinders, and pipes make them interesting to build.

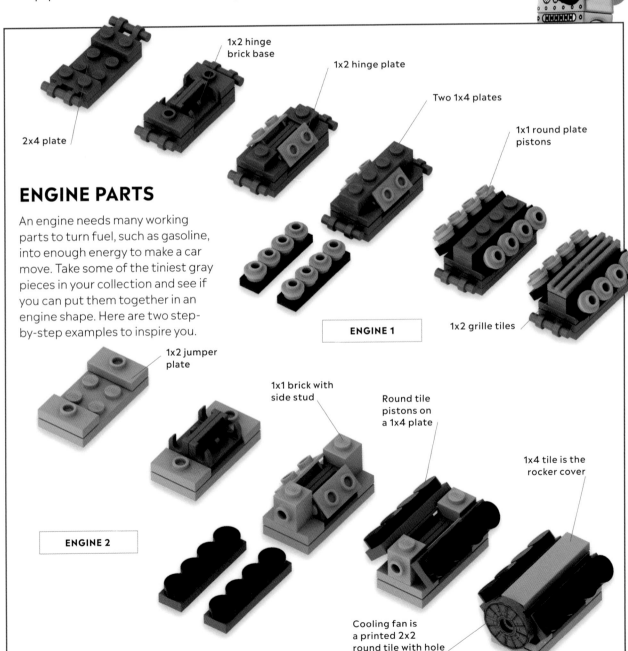

2x4 plate

1x2 hinge brick base

1x2 hinge plate

Two 1x4 plates

1x1 round plate pistons

ENGINE PARTS

An engine needs many working parts to turn fuel, such as gasoline, into enough energy to make a car move. Take some of the tiniest gray pieces in your collection and see if you can put them together in an engine shape. Here are two step-by-step examples to inspire you.

ENGINE 1

1x2 grille tiles

1x2 jumper plate

1x1 brick with side stud

Round tile pistons on a 1x4 plate

1x4 tile is the rocker cover

ENGINE 2

Cooling fan is a printed 2x2 round tile with hole

ENGINE PIECES

All kinds of small LEGO® pieces can be fitted together in different ways to create mechanical parts and machinery. Do you have any of these useful pieces in your collection?

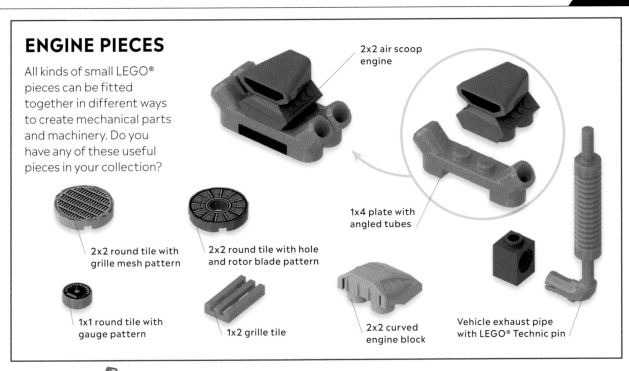

2x2 air scoop engine

1x4 plate with angled tubes

2x2 round tile with grille mesh pattern

2x2 round tile with hole and rotor blade pattern

1x1 round tile with gauge pattern

1x2 grille tile

2x2 curved engine block

Vehicle exhaust pipe with LEGO® Technic pin

HOT ROD ENGINE

The hot rod is a stripped-back car with an engine that isn't hidden by bodywork. The flaming "exposed" engine is made from layers of small pieces. The side details are held at an angle using plates with clips attached to bars. Learn more about this car on pages 68–69.

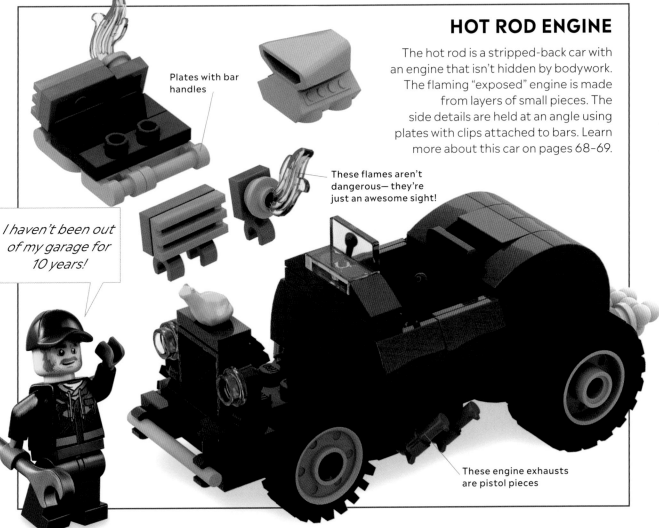

Plates with bar handles

These flames aren't dangerous— they're just an awesome sight!

I haven't been out of my garage for 10 years!

These engine exhausts are pistol pieces

QUAD BIKE

This heavy-duty four-wheeled vehicle can power through places most cars can't. Thick mud, steep hills, and rocky terrain are no trouble for a quad bike, but it can also join regular cars on roads. This quad bike has four extra-thick tires and protective bars on its front bumper.

My costume not only looks cool— it also provides padding in case I fall off!

Handlebar controls the steering

Bumper bar is one grille guard piece

Seat and mudguards are one piece

Four front headlights

Wide, off-road tire

ALL-BLACK BASE

The quad bike has a simple chassis built around one 2x6 plate. There are 2x2 plates with wheel-holding pins underneath it and plates with rails and clips above it. Unlike many car chassis, all of the pieces can be seen on the final build, so they're all black.

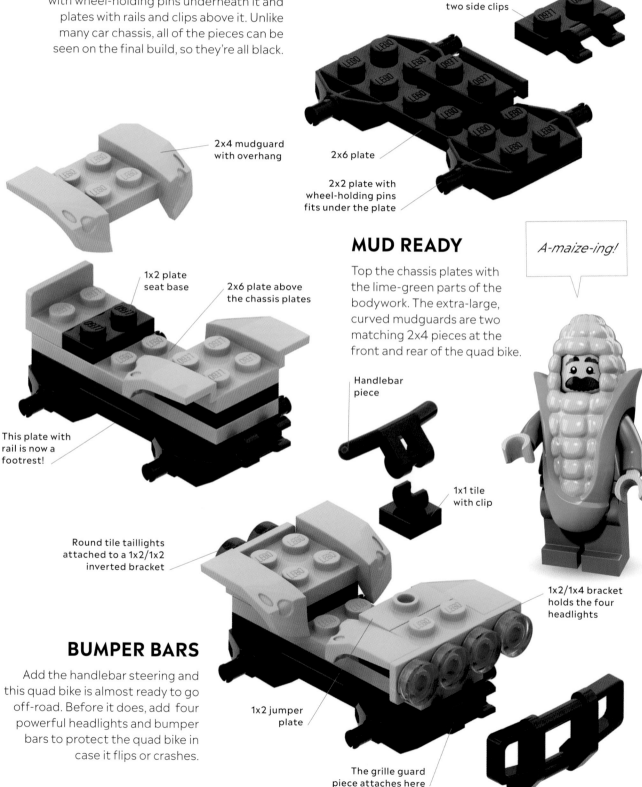

1x2 plate with rail

1x2 plate with two side clips

2x4 mudguard with overhang

2x6 plate

2x2 plate with wheel-holding pins fits under the plate

1x2 plate seat base

2x6 plate above the chassis plates

This plate with rail is now a footrest!

MUD READY

Top the chassis plates with the lime-green parts of the bodywork. The extra-large, curved mudguards are two matching 2x4 pieces at the front and rear of the quad bike.

A-maize-ing!

Handlebar piece

1x1 tile with clip

Round tile taillights attached to a 1x2/1x2 inverted bracket

1x2/1x4 bracket holds the four headlights

BUMPER BARS

Add the handlebar steering and this quad bike is almost ready to go off-road. Before it does, add four powerful headlights and bumper bars to protect the quad bike in case it flips or crashes.

1x2 jumper plate

The grille guard piece attaches here

GOLF CART

This little electric golf cart whizzes around the greens and fairways of golf courses, taking minifigures and their clubs all the way to the 18th hole. Built in a traditional black-and-white color scheme, there's room inside for one golfer and a club storage area at the back.

Flagpole is a bar attached to a brick with open stud

Anyone know a short putt to the 18th hole?

A 1x2 brick with hole forms the hole!

Two 1x4 tiles form the squared-off canopy

Golf club heads are 1x1 plates with side clips

Slope bricks create a rounded edge

Small 2x2 curved slope hood

A clip-and-bar connection holds the canopy frame at an angle

2x2 corner plate

1x3 tile

2x4 mudguard plate

2x1x1 curved slope

2x2 plate with wheel-holding pins

2x8 plate

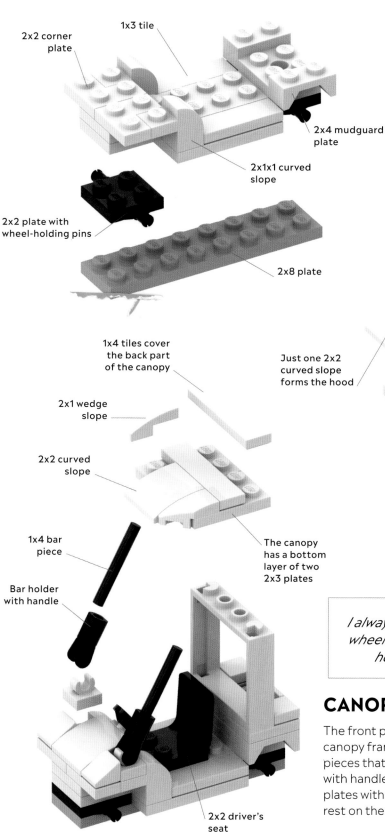

TEEING OFF

Golf carts mostly drive around on smooth surfaces, so their chassis can be low to the ground. A gray 2x8 plate locks the plates with wheel-holding pins on the bottom part of the chassis in place and also makes the base of the cart lower.

1x4x3 window piece is the rear frame

1x1 plate with side clip

Just one 2x2 curved slope forms the hood

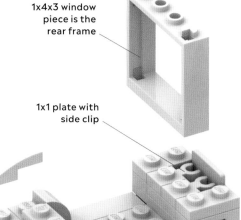

CLUB STORAGE

At the back of the golf cart is a storage area for two clubs, made from 1x1 plates with side clips. The rear frame of the cart, which is a window piece, attaches just in front of it.

1x4 tiles cover the back part of the canopy

2x1 wedge slope

2x2 curved slope

1x4 bar piece

Bar holder with handle

The canopy has a bottom layer of two 2x3 plates

2x2 driver's seat

I always take a spare wheel in case I get a hole in one.

CANOPY FRAME

The front part of the cart's canopy frame is made from bar pieces that fit into bar holders with handles. They attach to plates with clips at an angle and rest on the canopy at the top.

WHEELS AND CONNECTIONS

Without wheels, a car wouldn't be able to fulfill its purpose—to enjoy life on the open road! This book is filled with wheels and ideas for ways to connect them, but here are some particularly interesting or useful examples.

Find out more about the auto rickshaw on pages 24–25

THREE-WHEELER

The auto rickshaw shows two types of wheels and different ways to attach them. The solo front wheel clips onto a 2x2 plate with wheel holders, while the two back wheels slot onto a 2x2 plate with wheel holders.

The wheel fits between these two holders

Wheel center with stub axles

Smooth back tire and hubcap

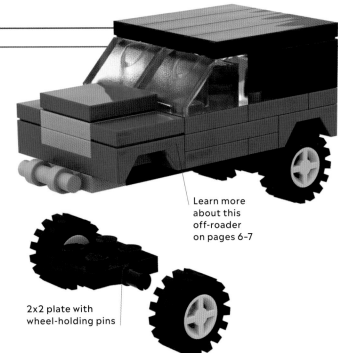

Learn more about this off-roader on pages 6-7

2x2 plate with wheel-holding pins

This tire has thick treads

SPARE TIRE

The off-roader is the only car in this book that has five wheels! It has a spare one attached to its rear, on a 1x2 plate with wheel-holding pin. The four other wheels use the same pin connection but on 2x2 plates.

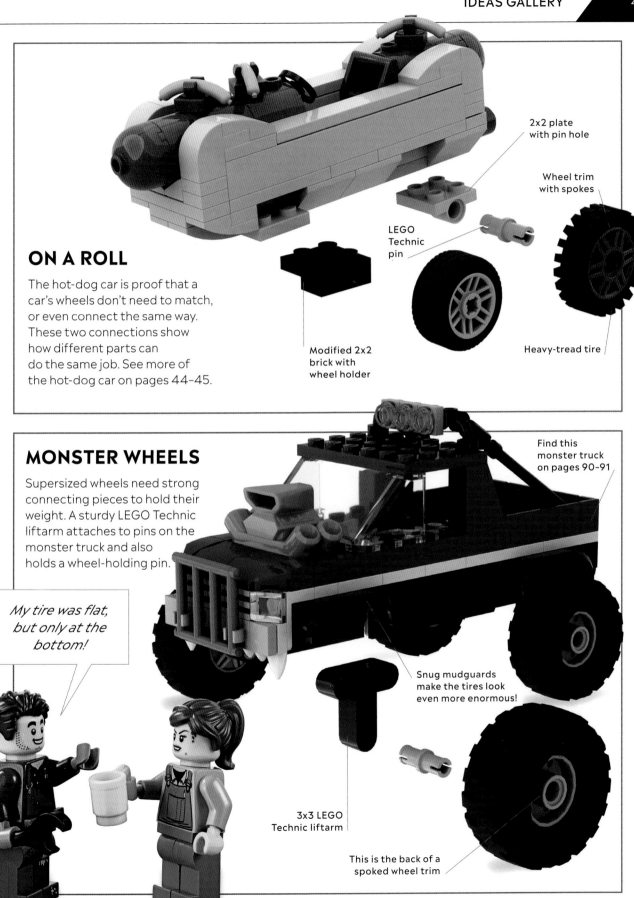

ON A ROLL

The hot-dog car is proof that a car's wheels don't need to match, or even connect the same way. These two connections show how different parts can do the same job. See more of the hot-dog car on pages 44–45.

2x2 plate with pin hole

Wheel trim with spokes

LEGO Technic pin

Heavy-tread tire

Modified 2x2 brick with wheel holder

MONSTER WHEELS

Supersized wheels need strong connecting pieces to hold their weight. A sturdy LEGO Technic liftarm attaches to pins on the monster truck and also holds a wheel-holding pin.

Find this monster truck on pages 90–91

My tire was flat, but only at the bottom!

Snug mudguards make the tires look even more enormous!

3x3 LEGO Technic liftarm

This is the back of a spoked wheel trim

RACING CAR

Your minifigures can live life in the fast lane in this racing car. Based on the vehicles used in big racing events such as Formula One, it has a single seat for the driver and an open cockpit. Its low, narrow shape allows it to reach high speeds while clinging to the twists and turns of the racetrack.

You still have a lap left to go!

I'd like to dedicate my win to my mother.

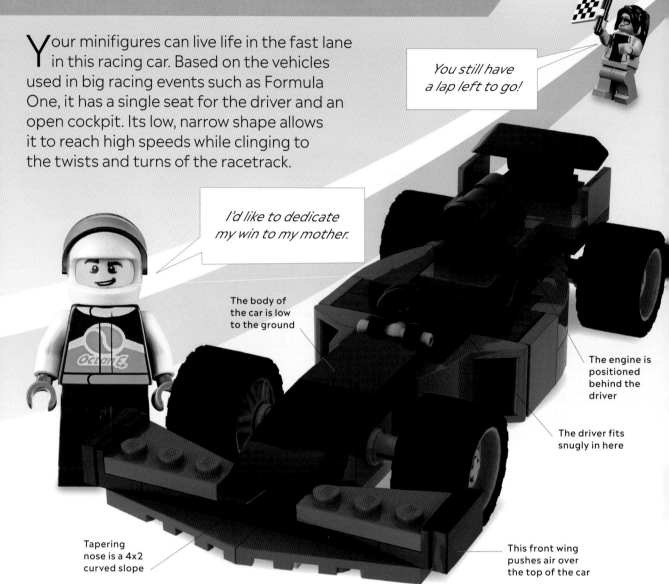

The body of the car is low to the ground

The engine is positioned behind the driver

The driver fits snugly in here

Tapering nose is a 4x2 curved slope

This front wing pushes air over the top of the car

5x2x1 bracket

1x2 LEGO Technic brick with hole

LEGO Technic axle

2x16 plate

LEGO Technic bushes stop the axles from moving

LIGHT AND FAST

A super-speedy car like this one needs a light chassis, with no heavy or unnecessary pieces. This minimal chassis is built around a 2x16 plate. Long LEGO Technic axles slide through bricks with holes on the chassis plate to provide places to attach the wheels on the final model.

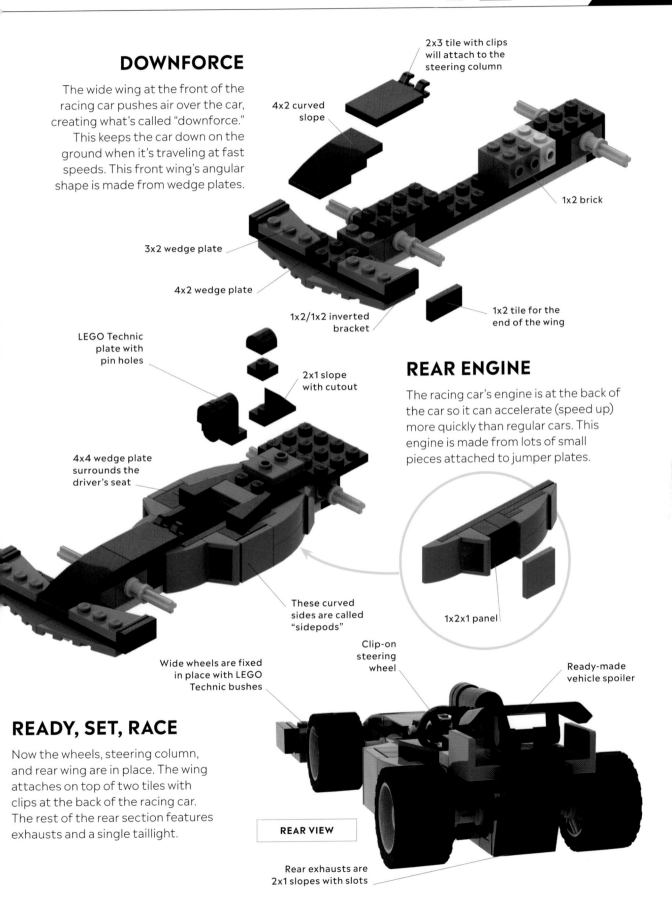

DOWNFORCE

The wide wing at the front of the racing car pushes air over the car, creating what's called "downforce." This keeps the car down on the ground when it's traveling at fast speeds. This front wing's angular shape is made from wedge plates.

2x3 tile with clips will attach to the steering column

4x2 curved slope

1x2 brick

3x2 wedge plate

4x2 wedge plate

1x2/1x2 inverted bracket

1x2 tile for the end of the wing

LEGO Technic plate with pin holes

2x1 slope with cutout

REAR ENGINE

The racing car's engine is at the back of the car so it can accelerate (speed up) more quickly than regular cars. This engine is made from lots of small pieces attached to jumper plates.

4x4 wedge plate surrounds the driver's seat

These curved sides are called "sidepods"

1x2x1 panel

Wide wheels are fixed in place with LEGO Technic bushes

Clip-on steering wheel

Ready-made vehicle spoiler

READY, SET, RACE

Now the wheels, steering column, and rear wing are in place. The wing attaches on top of two tiles with clips at the back of the racing car. The rest of the rear section features exhausts and a single taillight.

REAR VIEW

Rear exhausts are 2x1 slopes with slots

HOT-DOG CAR

M any people love hot dogs, but the owner of this car really, *really* loves hot dogs. With a curved bun base, a mustard-streaked sausage center, and ketchup and mustard exhausts, this car is no old banger!

It's not the wurst car I've owned.

Orange sausage pieces are mustard streaks!

Yellow 1x2 steering column and wheel

2x2 dome frankfurter end

2x1 curved slopes make a smooth bun shape

Ketchup and mustard-colored 1x1 round brick exhausts

BEGIN THE BUN

A car shaped like a long hot-dog bun needs a lengthy chassis base. The hot-dog car is built around a 2x10 plate. Double inverted slopes attached underneath the chassis plate give the bun base a curved look.

2x2 plate with wheel holder

2x2 plate with pin hole

The 2x10 plate can be any color

4x2 double inverted slope with cutout

RISING DOUGH

Build more plates on top of the lower part of the car to add height to the bun body. Then attach inverted curved slopes underneath the plates at the front of the car to give the bun its distinctive rounded end.

4x4 plate

The twin sauce exhausts will attach to this 1x2/1x2 bracket

2x1 inverted curved slope

2x4 plate

4x2 double inverted slope with cutout

Leave four studs for the minifigure driver

2x2x1 double curved slope

2x2x2/3 plate with two side studs

BUILD A BANGER

Once the bun bodywork is complete, it's time to build the sausage center of the hot-dog car. It's made from double curved slopes in the middle and round bricks and domes at the ends.

2x2 dome brick

An extra plate layer makes the sausage higher

I'm sorry, but I really mustard go.

2x1x1 curved slope

1x1 tile with clip

Steering wheel

FOOD TO GO

Add some more curves to the top edges of the car's bun body using curved slopes, then add a steering column. Serve up the hot-dog car with mustard stripes aptly made from mini hot-dog pieces attached to 1x1 tiles with clips.

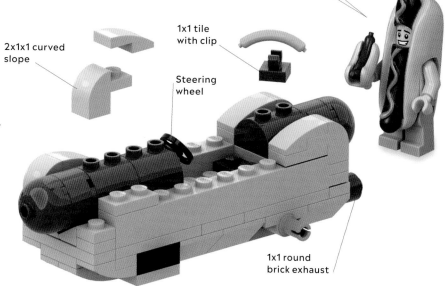

1x1 round brick exhaust

CHANGED-UP CARS

What happens if you take an ordinary looking car and modify it in different ways? By moving and changing just a few pieces at a time, you can customize and enhance your own existing car models.

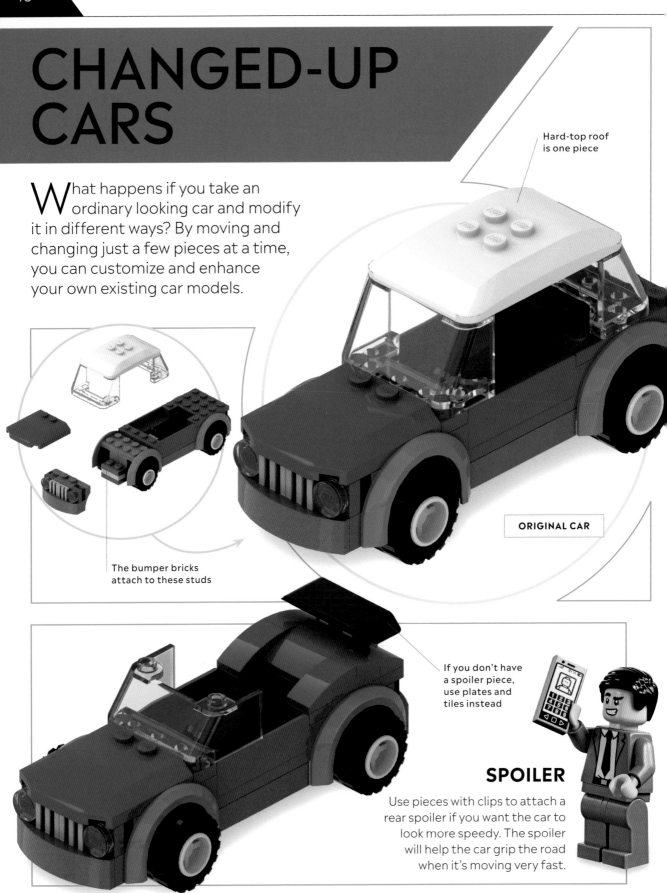

Hard-top roof is one piece

The bumper bricks attach to these studs

ORIGINAL CAR

If you don't have a spoiler piece, use plates and tiles instead

SPOILER

Use pieces with clips to attach a rear spoiler if you want the car to look more speedy. The spoiler will help the car grip the road when it's moving very fast.

RACING STRIPES

Change some of the hood and trunk pieces for white ones to create parallel racing stripes across the car's paintwork.

The hood is now made from three pieces instead of one

The stripes make it go faster!

White 2x1 curved slopes

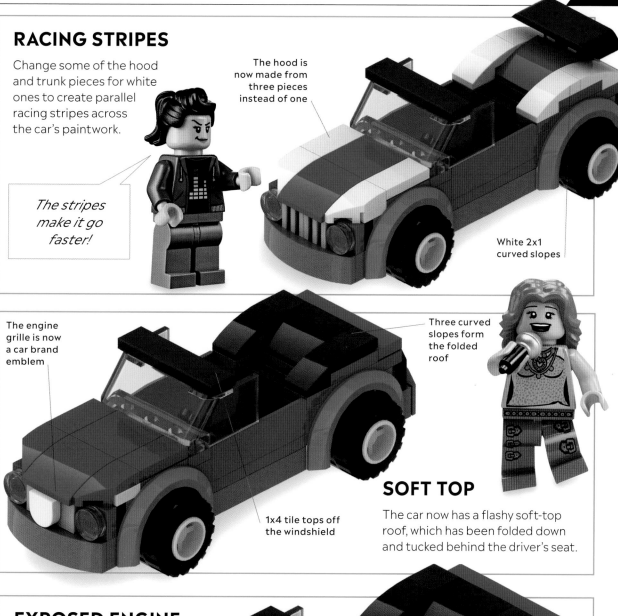

The engine grille is now a car brand emblem

Three curved slopes form the folded roof

1x4 tile tops off the windshield

SOFT TOP

The car now has a flashy soft-top roof, which has been folded down and tucked behind the driver's seat.

EXPOSED ENGINE

An exposed engine makes the car look extra powerful. But the driver may have a hard time seeing where they're going!

Large engine attaches to studs on original hood piece

BLACK CAB

Taxi! This black cab covers miles and miles of city streets each day, picking up passengers and taking them wherever they need to go. Its timeless black-and-chrome design features a light at the top that tells people the cab is available.

Hop in! The meter's running.

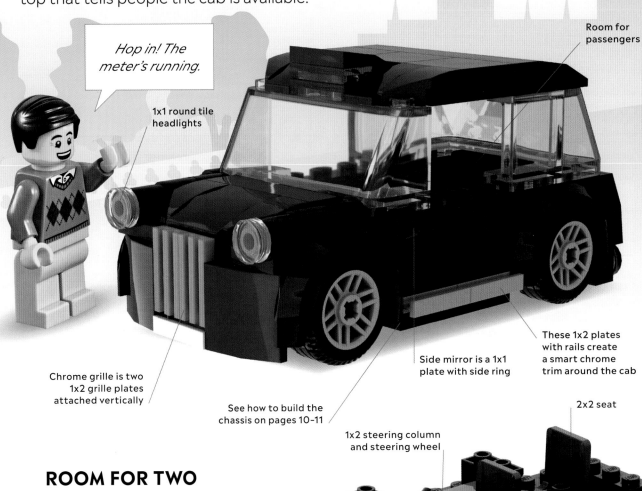

Room for passengers

1x1 round tile headlights

Chrome grille is two 1x2 grille plates attached vertically

See how to build the chassis on pages 10–11

Side mirror is a 1x1 plate with side ring

These 1x2 plates with rails create a smart chrome trim around the cab

ROOM FOR TWO

Taxi passengers usually sit behind the driver, so it's important to build two rows of seats inside. Place the front and rear seats inside your build at an early stage to ensure there's plenty of minifigure headroom and leg space.

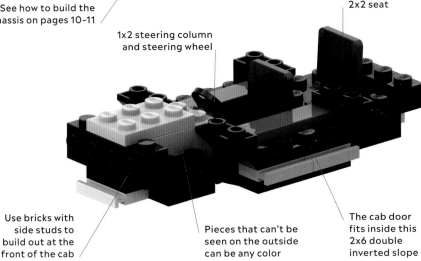

1x2 steering column and steering wheel

2x2 seat

Use bricks with side studs to build out at the front of the cab

Pieces that can't be seen on the outside can be any color

The cab door fits inside this 2x6 double inverted slope

BUILDING IN BLACK

The bodywork of the black cab is taking shape, with mudguards and pins for the wheels that are attached underneath the chassis. There are 1x4 brick doors and blue tile armrests for the driver.

Take me to LEGO City, please.

4x2 mudguard

1x4 tile armrest

1x4 brick door

This modified 2x4 brick with wheel pins fits under the chassis

2x2 curved slope

DISTINCTIVE DESIGN

The front section of a classic black cab has a unique shape. The cab's long, curved wings are made from small curved slopes and round bricks with holes, which the headlights slot inside. At the rear, the bumper is tall and flat.

This half pin is the base of the headlight

2x2 curved slope hood

1x1 double curved slope

2x2 curved slope

The roof has a bottom layer of plates

READY FOR SERVICE

Taxi passengers love to watch the city streets whizz by on their trips. Build a wide windshield and lots of windows around the seats before adding the roof. The taxi light is a 1x2 transparent orange tile on top of a plate in the same size and color.

2x6x2 windshield

1x2 tile

1x2x2 panel

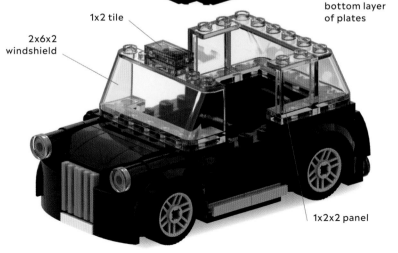

PICK-UP TRUCK

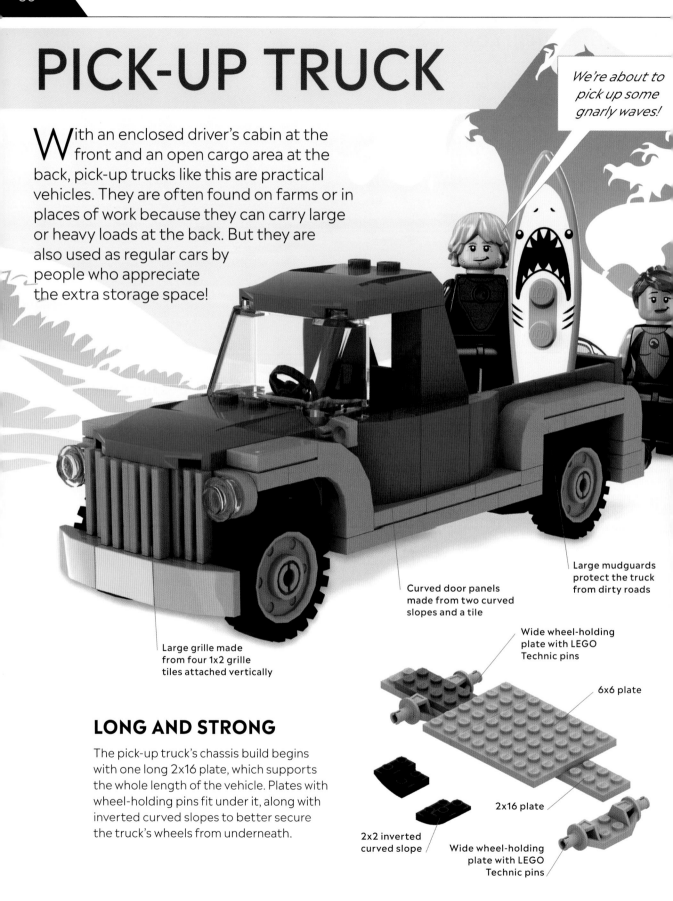

With an enclosed driver's cabin at the front and an open cargo area at the back, pick-up trucks like this are practical vehicles. They are often found on farms or in places of work because they can carry large or heavy loads at the back. But they are also used as regular cars by people who appreciate the extra storage space!

We're about to pick up some gnarly waves!

Large mudguards protect the truck from dirty roads

Curved door panels made from two curved slopes and a tile

Large grille made from four 1x2 grille tiles attached vertically

Wide wheel-holding plate with LEGO Technic pins

6x6 plate

2x16 plate

2x2 inverted curved slope

Wide wheel-holding plate with LEGO Technic pins

LONG AND STRONG

The pick-up truck's chassis build begins with one long 2x16 plate, which supports the whole length of the vehicle. Plates with wheel-holding pins fit under it, along with inverted curved slopes to better secure the truck's wheels from underneath.

OPEN AND CLOSED

Now it's possible to see where the two areas of the pick-up truck will be built up. A 6x4 plate at the back will become the open cargo area. The smaller plates at the front form the base of the enclosed driver's cabin.

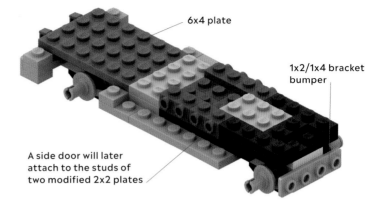

6x4 plate

1x2/1x4 bracket bumper

A side door will later attach to the studs of two modified 2x2 plates

2x2 round plates make the cargo area higher

1x4 tile tops the mudguard

Steering wheel and stand

1x2 brick with side studs

Smooth tiles for the running boards

2x2 curved slopes make the doors rounded

RUNNING BOARDS

The pick-up now has wide running boards all along its sides. These protect the truck from any dirt and stones the wheels might kick up. At this stage, also add the wide side doors of the driver's cabin and build the bumpers.

1x2 tile license plate

1x2 rounded plate

Two 2x2 corner plates

Tailgate has click hinges at the bottom

1x2x1 panels are the sides of the cargo area

The roof will rest on these 2x1x2 slope bricks

2x1x1 curved slope

1x1 round plate headlight

ENGINE GRILLE

A giant engine grille is a classic feature of a pick-up truck. It needs to be large so a lot of air can get to the hardworking engine. This pick-up truck's grille is built from 1x2 grille tiles, plates, and rounded plates.

The ends of 1x2 hinge plates make good side mirrors!

SWITCHED-UP PICK-UPS

The pick-up truck on pages 50–51 can be reimagined in multiple ways. Look at the pieces in your collection and think about how you could modify your models to add extra tools and functions, create different looks, or turn them into something else entirely.

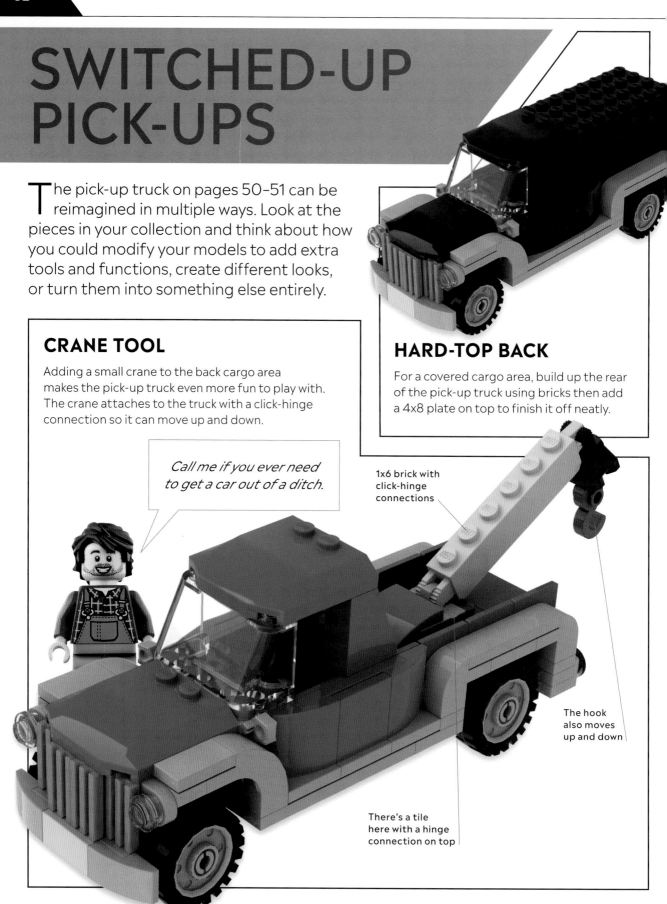

CRANE TOOL

Adding a small crane to the back cargo area makes the pick-up truck even more fun to play with. The crane attaches to the truck with a click-hinge connection so it can move up and down.

HARD-TOP BACK

For a covered cargo area, build up the rear of the pick-up truck using bricks then add a 4x8 plate on top to finish it off neatly.

Call me if you ever need to get a car out of a ditch.

1x6 brick with click-hinge connections

The hook also moves up and down

There's a tile here with a hinge connection on top

SOUND SYSTEM

This pick-up truck has been turned into a stage on wheels, for concerts on the go! Removing the sides creates room for a minifigure performer as well as two large speakers and a microphone.

Speaker base made from three plates

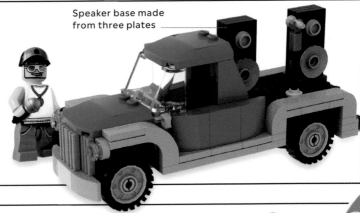

RUSTY PAINT

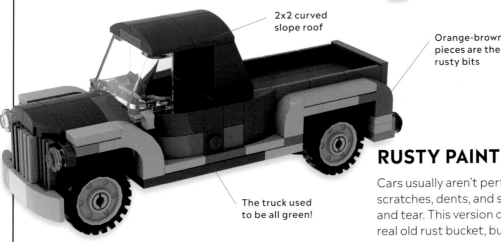

2x2 curved slope roof

Orange-brown pieces are the rusty bits

The truck used to be all green!

Cars usually aren't perfect—they often have scratches, dents, and signs of rust from wear and tear. This version of the pick-up truck is a real old rust bucket, but somebody loves it!

HOT ROD

Like the hot rod car on pages 68–69, the pick-up truck has now been stripped back and rebuilt with a roaring exposed engine and flaming and lightning sides.

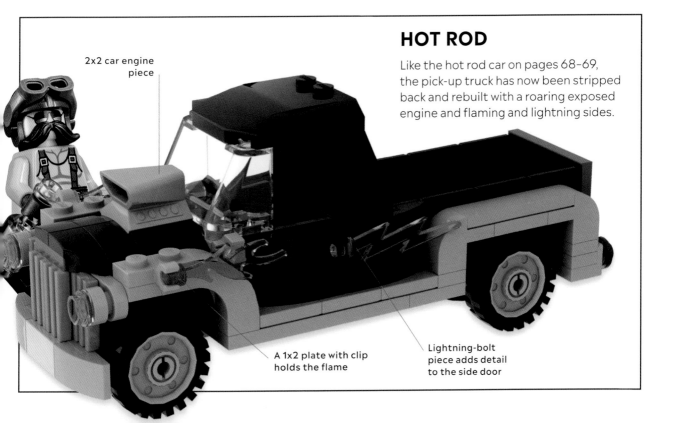

2x2 car engine piece

A 1x2 plate with clip holds the flame

Lightning-bolt piece adds detail to the side door

BRICK CAR

It does 0 to 60 bricks in seconds.

Ever thought of turning your favorite LEGO bricks into automobiles? The classic 2x4 brick inspired this set of wheels. There are studs at the front and back and there's room in the middle for a LEGO obsessed driver. Brick-themed costumes are optional!

I'm very attached to this car.

3x6x1 curved windshield

Four curved slopes for the smooth backrest

2x2 round tile "stud"

1x2 tile license plate

Round mudguard pie[...]

Build a tiny version from three layers of plates!

1x4 plate

4x12 plate

1x6 plate

Skateboard wheels

2x2 modified plate with wheel holder

1x2/1x2 bracket

1x2 grille tile

These plate[...] form the low[...] sides of the [...]

CHASSIS VIEW

A brick-inspired car like this one needs a solid, boxy base. Its chassis is a narrow 2x12 plate with shorter plates and wheel holders attached horizontally across it. A 4x12 plate with mudguard pieces then forms the second layer of the brick car.

HIDDEN ENGINE

If you peek under the hood of a real car, you will find an engine. The brick car may be made from LEGO pieces, but it's no different! There's a 2x2 car engine piece built into the bricklike hood, behind the bumper.

This piece is a mudguard on many other cars

4x1 double curved slope

The rear bumper is the same as the front one

2x2 car engine piece

1x2 tile license plate

The bumper fits onto 1x2/1x2 brackets

This 1x1 plate will fit under the driver's seat

More small plates fill gaps below the top layer

2x6 plate

LEVELING OFF

Now the brick car has the dimensions of a classic 2x4 brick. The body of the car has been leveled off with small plates, leaving a big square hole in the middle for the minifigure driver's cabin.

2x1 curved slope

2x2 corner plate

2x1x1 curved slopes form a rounded backrest

2x2 tile

2x2 plate

Studs attach to 1x1 plates

SUPERSIZED STUDS

The brick car wouldn't look like its LEGO namesake without studs! There are two at the front and two at the back of the car, made from 2x2 round plates and tiles. In the middle, where two more studs might go on a real 2x4 brick, build in a plush driver's seat and a joystick for steering.

Tiles top off the bodywork

SPORTS CAR

Your minifigures can feel the wind in their LEGO® hair in this convertible sports car! Its soft-top roof, made from black tiles and slopes, can be removed for top-down driving on sunny days. Built for speed, this sleek vehicle is small and low to the ground, with white racing stripes on the hood.

2x4 tiles complete the soft-top roof

Two 3x2 slopes form the base of the roof

1x2 curved slope stripe

Smoked glass 3x4x1 windshield piece

2x1 curved slope bumper

1x4 brick door

Transparent 1x1 slope is a headlight lens

That's one sturdy-looking chassis.

BODY BASE

The sports car body is built around one chassis piece. Plates and bricks are then added on top, underneath, and on the sides. If you don't have a chassis piece like this, you could make your own using plates. Look at pages 10–11 for lots of chassis-building ideas.

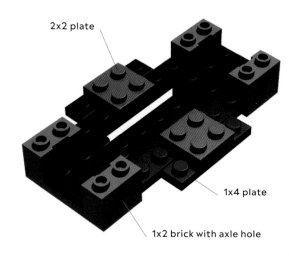

2x2 plate

1x4 plate

1x2 brick with axle hole

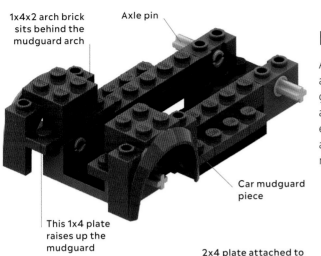

1x4x2 arch brick sits behind the mudguard arch

Axle pin

Car mudguard piece

This 1x4 plate raises up the mudguard

HIGH WHEELS

A speedy sports car needs a body that's low to the ground so it can move fast and make sharp turns with ease. To keep the chassis low, attach the wheel axles and mudguards slightly above it.

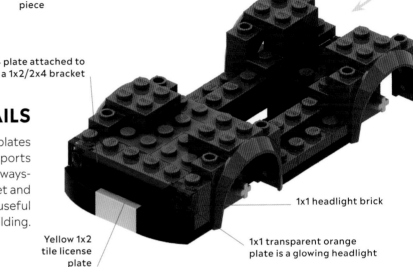

2x4 plate attached to a 1x2/2x4 bracket

1x1 headlight brick

1x1 transparent orange plate is a glowing headlight

Yellow 1x2 tile license plate

BUMPER DETAILS

The headlights and license plates at the front and rear of the sports car are attached using sideways-building techniques. Bracket and headlight bricks are especially useful for sideways or SNOT building.

1x1 tile extends the racing stripe

The windshield attaches here

SMOOTH RIDE

Curved slopes and small tiles form the sports car's smooth, racing-striped hood. Several curved slope pieces above the back bumper continue the sleek curves at the rear.

It's a top-down kind of day!

1x4 tile

2x4 tile is the folded-down roof

2x1 wedge slope

1x2 grille tile

1x1 transparent orange plate brake light

REAR VIEW

1x2 curved slope

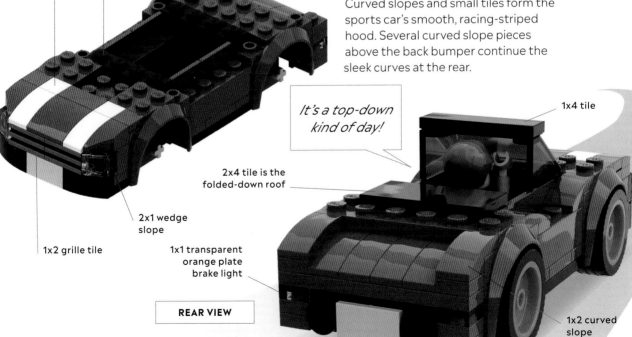

MICROSCALE VEHICLES

These mini vehicles are fun to build from a small number of tiny bricks. They're all microscale, which means smaller than minifigure scale. At microscale, a 1x2 tile can become a whole car hood, two 1x1 cheese slopes are a windshield, and skateboard wheels are full-sized tires.

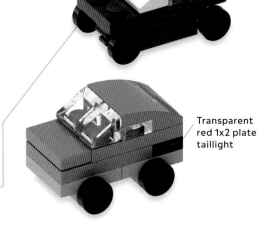

The roof is one 2x2 curved slope

Transparent red 1x2 plate taillight

Two 1x1 cheese slopes are the tailfin

CARS

These cars may be small but they have lots of detail. The blue car has a tailfin for a 1950s look, the orange one has little red tail lights, and the pink car's body is low to the ground.

TRUCKS

These trucks have even more interesting details to make them instantly recognizable. They're built to carry ice cream, pizza, and extra-large chickens!

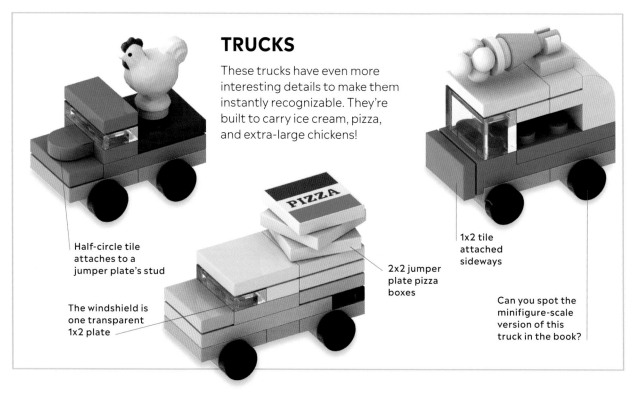

Half-circle tile attaches to a jumper plate's stud

The windshield is one transparent 1x2 plate

PIZZA

2x2 jumper plate pizza boxes

1x2 tile attached sideways

Can you spot the minifigure-scale version of this truck in the book?

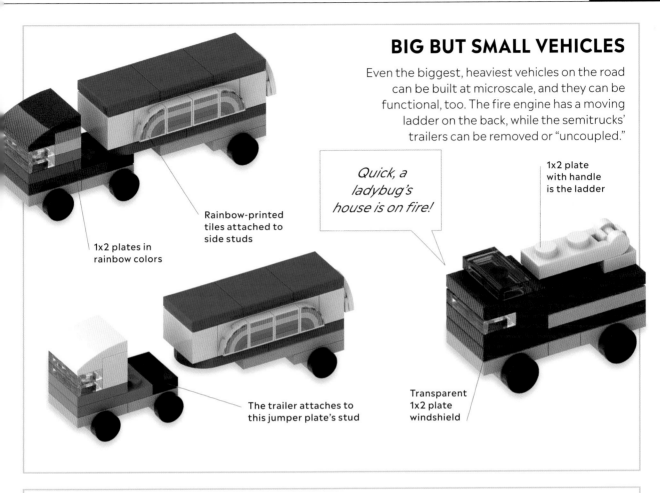

BIG BUT SMALL VEHICLES

Even the biggest, heaviest vehicles on the road can be built at microscale, and they can be functional, too. The fire engine has a moving ladder on the back, while the semitrucks' trailers can be removed or "uncoupled."

Quick, a ladybug's house is on fire!

1x2 plate with handle is the ladder

Rainbow-printed tiles attached to side studs

1x2 plates in rainbow colors

The trailer attaches to this jumper plate's stud

Transparent 1x2 plate windshield

COPY YOUR BUILDS

Why not try making microscale versions of your favorite builds? This mini 4x4 has all the details of its larger four-wheeled friend (which can be seen in more detail on pages 6-7).

It's like having a baby!

This model is double the size of the microscale version

Two cheese slopes for the windshield

2x2 tile soft-top roof

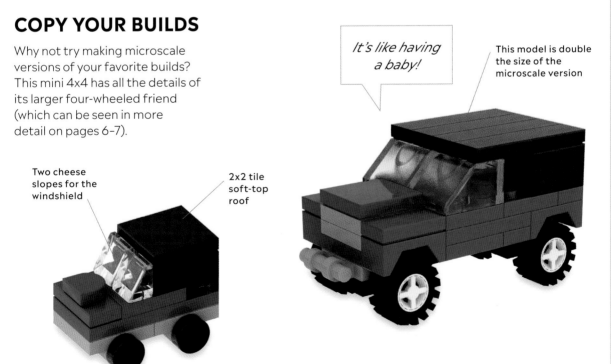

UNDERWATER CAR

There are roads all over the land, but much of the ocean is unexplored—until now! This propeller-powered aquatic automobile is built to roam the ocean floor. The underwater car's two watertight seats have big bubble windows so its driver and his small passenger can get a 360-degree view of the passing marine life.

I bought this car for shellfish reasons, but the boy seems to like it, too.

Smaller rear seat and window

Bubble window is a half sphere windshield

Thick-tread tires for moving through sand

Life buoy and flipper door handle

Snorkel bumper with bubbles

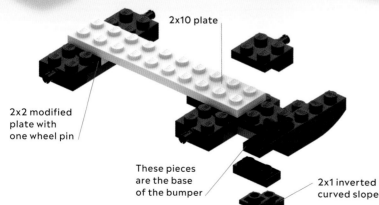

2x10 plate

2x2 modified plate with one wheel pin

These pieces are the base of the bumper

2x1 inverted curved slope

SANDY CHASSIS

The underwater car has a high chassis because it spends most of its time navigating deep-water dunes.
It's built around a 2x10 plate. Plates with wheel-holding pins fit to smaller plates underneath it, so the chassis plate is higher than the wheel pins.

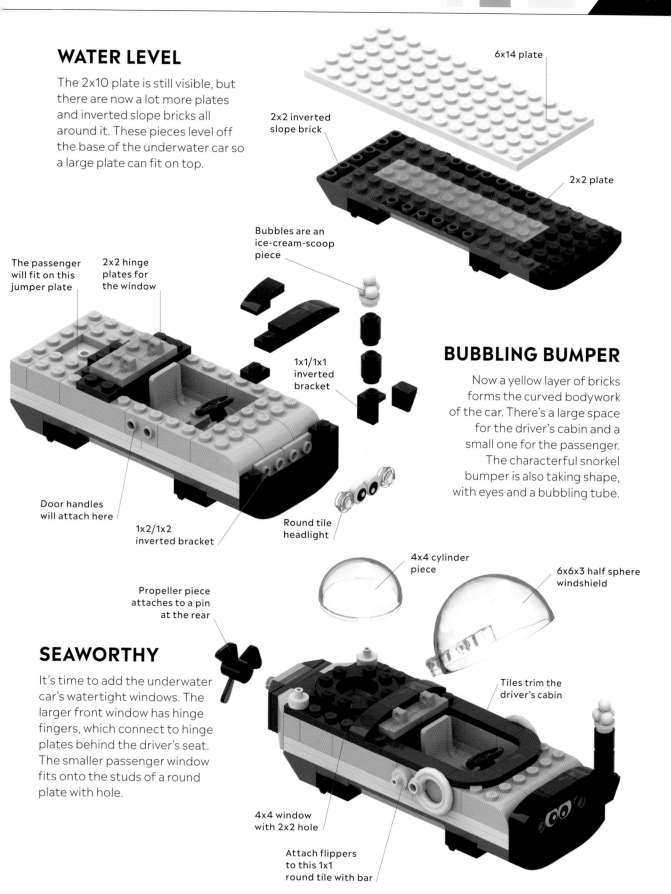

WATER LEVEL

The 2x10 plate is still visible, but there are now a lot more plates and inverted slope bricks all around it. These pieces level off the base of the underwater car so a large plate can fit on top.

6x14 plate

2x2 inverted slope brick

2x2 plate

Bubbles are an ice-cream-scoop piece

The passenger will fit on this jumper plate

2x2 hinge plates for the window

1x1/1x1 inverted bracket

BUBBLING BUMPER

Now a yellow layer of bricks forms the curved bodywork of the car. There's a large space for the driver's cabin and a small one for the passenger. The characterful snorkel bumper is also taking shape, with eyes and a bubbling tube.

Door handles will attach here

1x2/1x2 inverted bracket

Round tile headlight

4x4 cylinder piece

6x6x3 half sphere windshield

Propeller piece attaches to a pin at the rear

SEAWORTHY

It's time to add the underwater car's watertight windows. The larger front window has hinge fingers, which connect to hinge plates behind the driver's seat. The smaller passenger window fits onto the studs of a round plate with hole.

Tiles trim the driver's cabin

4x4 window with 2x2 hole

Attach flippers to this 1x1 round tile with bar

DRIVERLESS CAR

This is one clever car! Driverless or self-driving cars like this don't need a driver because they can plan a driving route, read road signs, and sense the environment around them. This build has an access ramp and plenty of room inside for someone in a wheelchair.

The large back door opens at the top

Look, no hands!

Six curved slopes form the short hood

1x1 cheese slope side mirror

Simple 1x1 round tile headlights

Small, smooth tires

BUILT-IN RAMP

The low base of the driverless car has a first layer of a 4x8 plate with lots of smaller plates on top to make it six studs wide. A row of curved slopes at one end forms the ramp for getting in and out of the vehicle.

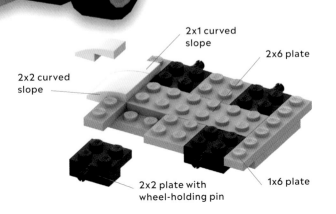

2x1 curved slope

2x6 plate

2x2 curved slope

2x2 plate with wheel-holding pin

1x6 plate

CAR FLOOR

Add tiles on top of the chassis layers to create a smooth car floor. The cheese slopes in the floor will stop a wheelchair from rolling too far forward when the car is moving.

2x4 tile

1x1 cheese slope

The side door will attach to this 1x8 plate

2x4 plate

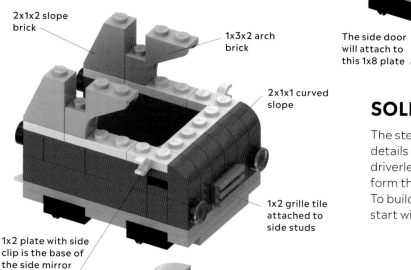

2x1x2 slope brick

1x3x2 arch brick

2x1x1 curved slope

1x2 grille tile attached to side studs

1x2 plate with side clip is the base of the side mirror

SOLID DESIGN

The steeply sloping hood and bumper details are now in place at the front of the driverless car, and bricks of different sizes form the solid sides of the bodywork. To build the top part of the car's frame, start with slope bricks and arches.

1x2 plate with clip

4x6 plate door

1x2 plate with bar handle with closed sides

4x6x2 curved wedge roof

2x2 plate

UNDERSIDE VIEW

REAR DOOR

Finish the car with a smooth roof and add a rear door. This one has clip-and-bar hinges at the top so they do not take up space near the doorway ramp.

2x2 curved slopes hide the door hinges

x6x2 windshield

Round tile taillight

The cheese slope side mirror attaches here

Where shall I go today?

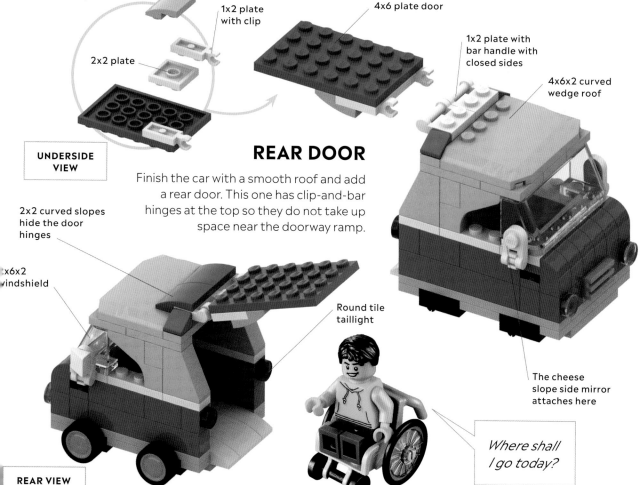

REAR VIEW

DISPLAYING YOUR CARS

I f you've built a LEGO car you're particularly proud of, you might want to build somewhere to display or park it when you're not playing with it. Your favorite car could be floating, floodlit, or posing next to a cityscape. What a show-off!

FLOATING DISPLAY

A LEGO car can rest on the 2x4 brick at the top of this small, angled holder and look like it's floating. The brick is at an angle thanks to a hinge-brick-and-plate connection underneath it.

1x2 hinge brick base

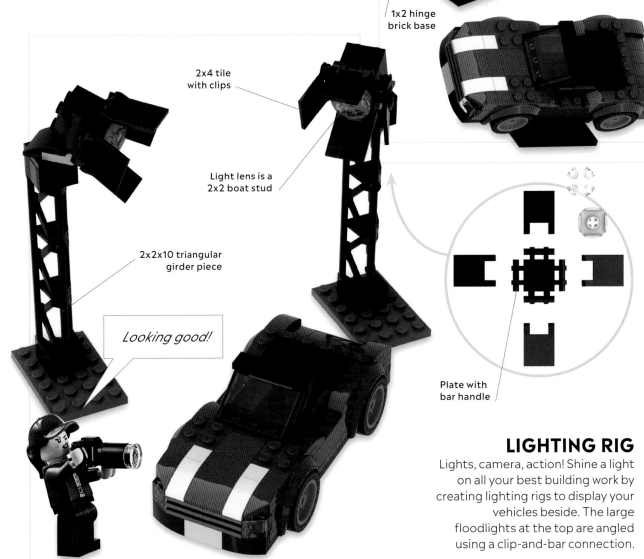

2x4 tile with clips

Light lens is a 2x2 boat stud

2x2x10 triangular girder piece

Looking good!

Plate with bar handle

LIGHTING RIG

Lights, camera, action! Shine a light on all your best building work by creating lighting rigs to display your vehicles beside. The large floodlights at the top are angled using a clip-and-bar connection.

PLINTH

You could build a simple block or plinth to display your most awesome automobiles on. This one has one large 8x16 tile on the top, but you could use smaller tiles to create the same effect.

Plates in various sizes around the edges

1x2 slope sides

8x16 tile

LANDSCAPE

Build a hilly microscale backdrop where your cars can park up and enjoy the view! You can make any kind of landscape next to a smooth road surface. You could even theme your scenes around your favorite car designs.

Rolling curved slope hills

1x1 cone fir trees

CITYSCAPE

City-based cars will look super sophisticated next to a microscale cityscape. They may even want to take a selfie! The tiny skyscrapers are made from alternating opaque and transparent tiles.

Transparent 1x2 plate

Cheese slope rooftops

Where did it go?

2x2 tile road surface

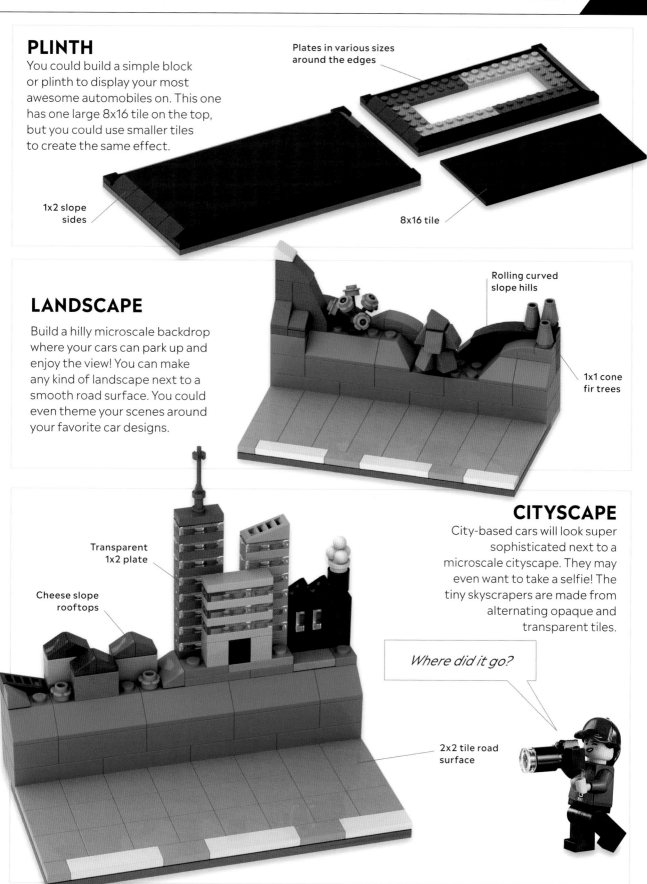

CLOUD CAR

N ot all cars need to be built for the road. This imaginary flying car floats high among the clouds, spreading color and cheer instead of gas fumes from its rainbow exhaust! It looks just like a fluffy cloud, thanks to its rounded shape and white-and-aqua color scheme.

Perhaps I can let go of this balloon now....

Transparent 1x2x1 panel is a tiny windshield

Tiles and plates in rainbow colors for the exhaust

2x2 round tiles attached on the side enhance the round, fluffy shape

1x1 double curved slopes make a curved bumper

4x8 plate

2x1 curved slope

FIRST CURVES

The base of the cloud car isn't as fluffy-looking as the exterior—it's one rectangular 4x8 plate. But the cloud curves are already starting to appear, with the addition of curved slopes underneath the front and back of the chassis.

2x2 curved slope

Thin 2x2 plate with tiny wheels

GATHERING CLOUDS

Keep building on top and below the car's base to build up the cloud shape, incorporating bricks with side studs to attach sideways pieces to later. Also build a plate with handle into the rear of the car—this will hold the rainbow exhaust.

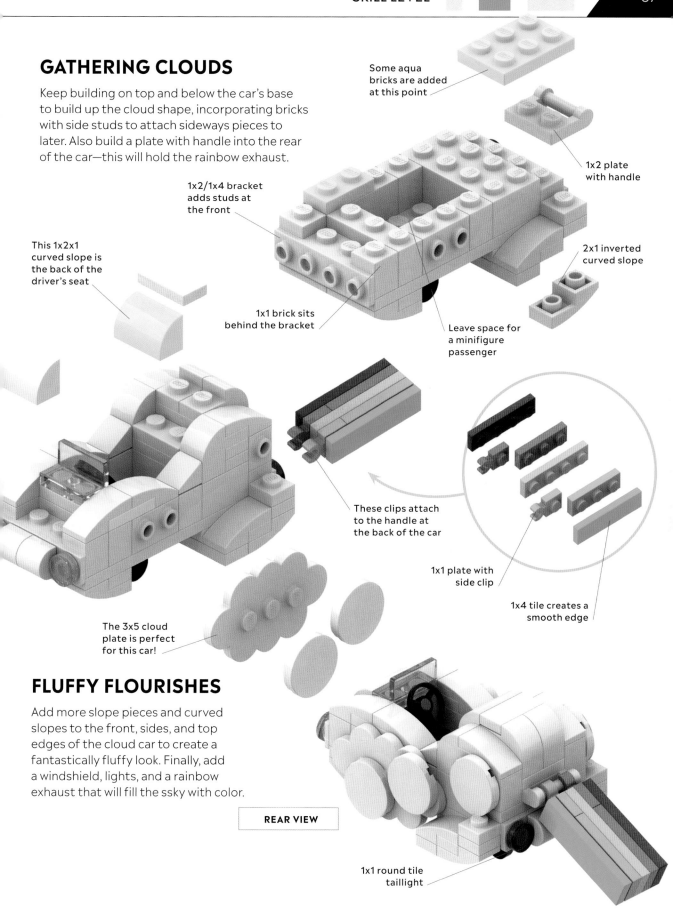

Some aqua bricks are added at this point

1x2 plate with handle

1x2/1x4 bracket adds studs at the front

This 1x2x1 curved slope is the back of the driver's seat

2x1 inverted curved slope

1x1 brick sits behind the bracket

Leave space for a minifigure passenger

These clips attach to the handle at the back of the car

1x1 plate with side clip

1x4 tile creates a smooth edge

The 3x5 cloud plate is perfect for this car!

FLUFFY FLOURISHES

Add more slope pieces and curved slopes to the front, sides, and top edges of the cloud car to create a fantastically fluffy look. Finally, add a windshield, lights, and a rainbow exhaust that will fill the ssky with color.

REAR VIEW

1x1 round tile taillight

HOT ROD

A hot rod is usually an older car that's been stripped back and rebuilt to be even faster and cooler than it was before. This one looks revved up and ready to race with its huge engine, flames, and fearsome froggy figurehead!

> I use any extra engine oil on my hair.

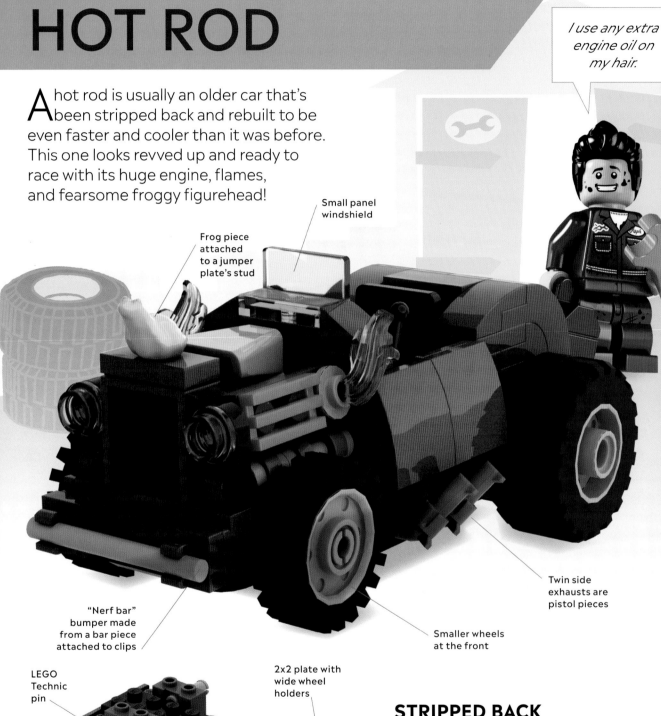

Small panel windshield

Frog piece attached to a jumper plate's stud

"Nerf bar" bumper made from a bar piece attached to clips

Smaller wheels at the front

Twin side exhausts are pistol pieces

LEGO Technic pin

2x2 plate with wide wheel holders

LEGO Technic 2x4 brick with holes

Inverted curved slopes lock the wheel holders in place

STRIPPED BACK

Hot rod-owning minifigures love to strip cars right back to their bases like this. The hot rod's chassis is built around a 2x12 plate. There are different wheel-holding parts at the front and the back to accommodate the different-sized wheels.

EXPOSED BUMPER

On a hot rod, parts that are usually built within the car are outside it, or exposed. This hot rod has exposed headlights on the front bumper above a "nerf bar," which is a metal rod that acts like a bumper.

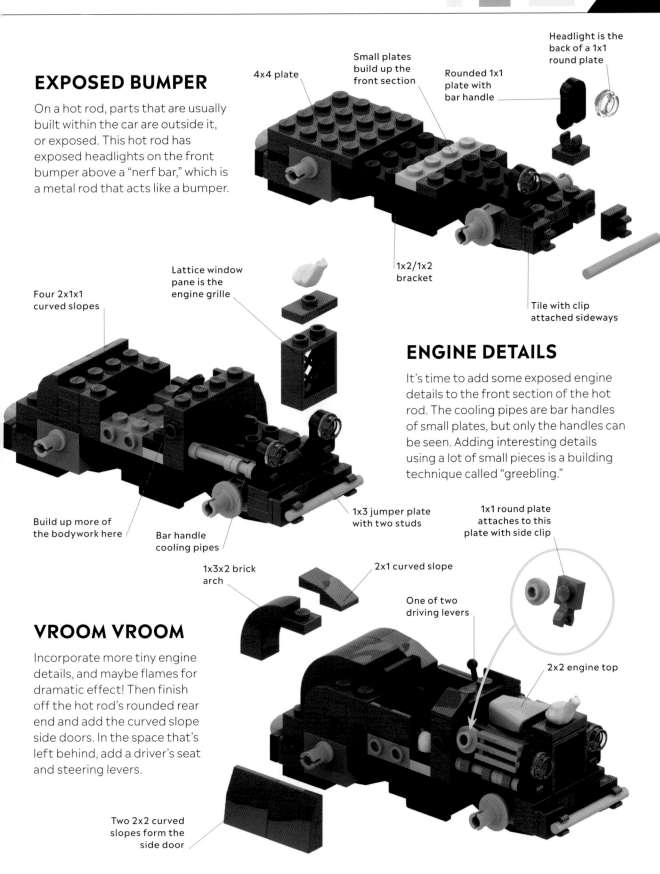

4x4 plate

Small plates build up the front section

Rounded 1x1 plate with bar handle

Headlight is the back of a 1x1 round plate

1x2/1x2 bracket

Tile with clip attached sideways

Four 2x1x1 curved slopes

Lattice window pane is the engine grille

ENGINE DETAILS

It's time to add some exposed engine details to the front section of the hot rod. The cooling pipes are bar handles of small plates, but only the handles can be seen. Adding interesting details using a lot of small pieces is a building technique called "greebling."

Build up more of the bodywork here

Bar handle cooling pipes

1x3 jumper plate with two studs

1x1 round plate attaches to this plate with side clip

1x3x2 brick arch

2x1 curved slope

One of two driving levers

2x2 engine top

VROOM VROOM

Incorporate more tiny engine details, and maybe flames for dramatic effect! Then finish off the hot rod's rounded rear end and add the curved slope side doors. In the space that's left behind, add a driver's seat and steering levers.

Two 2x2 curved slopes form the side door

MAKING ROADS

If you're tired of pushing your LEGO car creations over carpets and tables, build them smooth roads to drive around on! Here are some building ideas for roads as well as interesting features on and around them, such as sidewalks, bike lanes, and crosswalks.

TILE ROADS

You can build smooth tile roads on top of plates. The plates underneath can be any size, as they'll be covered by the tile road surface. But you could leave some plates exposed so you can attach trees, plants, and other roadside items to them.

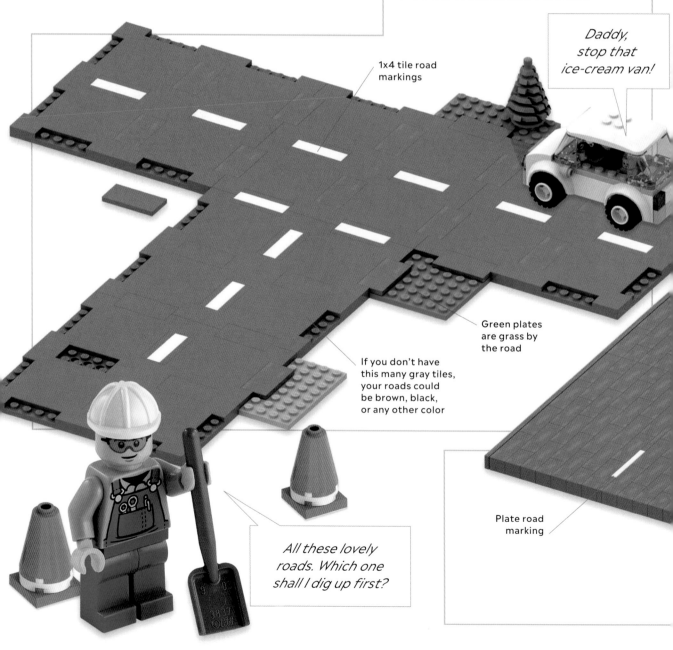

1x4 tile road markings

Daddy, stop that ice-cream van!

Green plates are grass by the road

If you don't have this many gray tiles, your roads could be brown, black, or any other color

Plate road marking

All these lovely roads. Which one shall I dig up first?

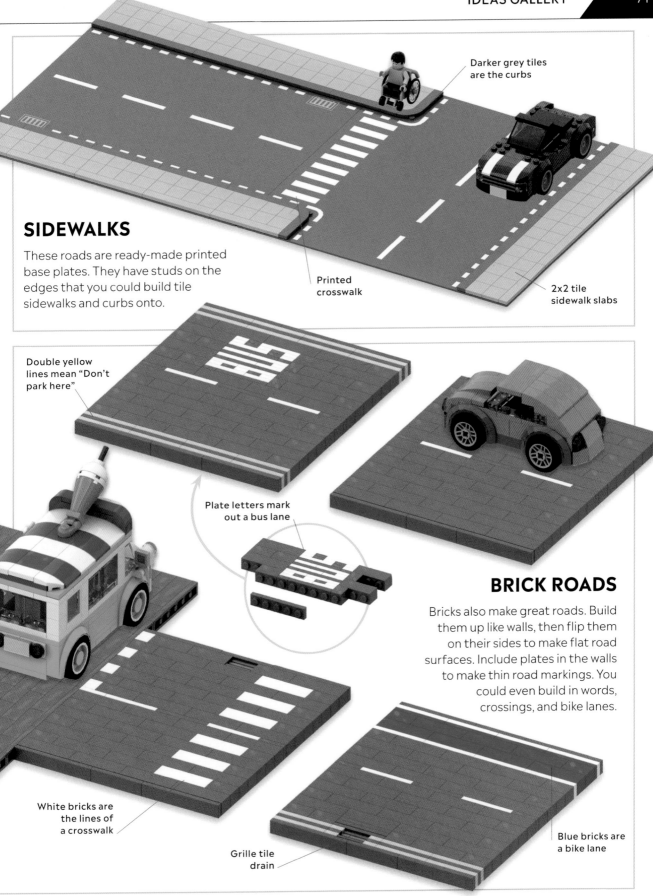

SIDEWALKS

These roads are ready-made printed base plates. They have studs on the edges that you could build tile sidewalks and curbs onto.

Darker grey tiles are the curbs

Printed crosswalk

2x2 tile sidewalk slabs

Double yellow lines mean "Don't park here"

Plate letters mark out a bus lane

BRICK ROADS

Bricks also make great roads. Build them up like walls, then flip them on their sides to make flat road surfaces. Include plates in the walls to make thin road markings. You could even build in words, crossings, and bike lanes.

White bricks are the lines of a crosswalk

Grille tile drain

Blue bricks are a bike lane

PIRATE CAR

Shiver me timbers! Is it a car? Is it a boat? It's both! A pirate's life may be mostly spent at sea, but when a salty seadog needs to be a landlubber like the rest of us, this pirate car has everything they need to feel at home. There's a wide deck, ship's wheel steering, and a scary-looking sail.

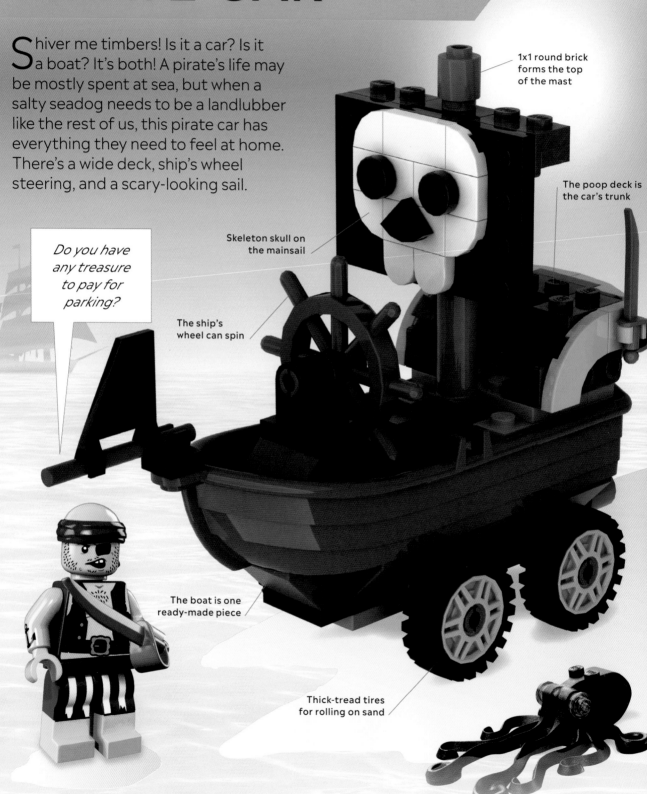

Do you have any treasure to pay for parking?

1x1 round brick forms the top of the mast

The poop deck is the car's trunk

Skeleton skull on the mainsail

The ship's wheel can spin

The boat is one ready-made piece

Thick-tread tires for rolling on sand

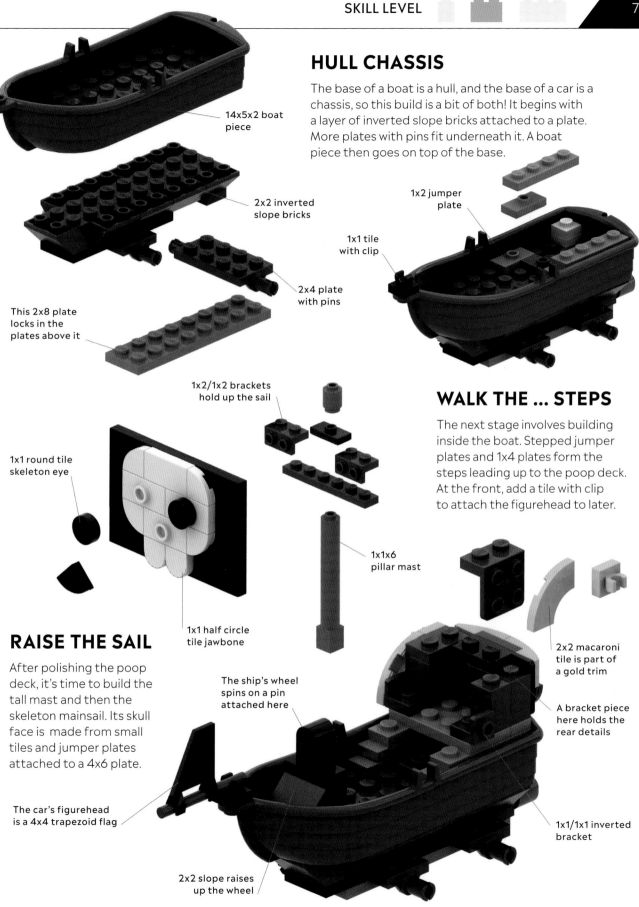

HULL CHASSIS

The base of a boat is a hull, and the base of a car is a chassis, so this build is a bit of both! It begins with a layer of inverted slope bricks attached to a plate. More plates with pins fit underneath it. A boat piece then goes on top of the base.

14x5x2 boat piece

2x2 inverted slope bricks

This 2x8 plate locks in the plates above it

2x4 plate with pins

1x2 jumper plate

1x1 tile with clip

WALK THE ... STEPS

The next stage involves building inside the boat. Stepped jumper plates and 1x4 plates form the steps leading up to the poop deck. At the front, add a tile with clip to attach the figurehead to later.

1x2/1x2 brackets hold up the sail

1x1 round tile skeleton eye

1x1 half circle tile jawbone

1x1x6 pillar mast

2x2 macaroni tile is part of a gold trim

A bracket piece here holds the rear details

RAISE THE SAIL

After polishing the poop deck, it's time to build the tall mast and then the skeleton mainsail. Its skull face is made from small tiles and jumper plates attached to a 4x6 plate.

The ship's wheel spins on a pin attached here

The car's figurehead is a 4x4 trapezoid flag

1x1/1x1 inverted bracket

2x2 slope raises up the wheel

YELLOW TAXI

You can't miss this bright yellow taxi cab. Hail one of these and it'll take you anywhere you need to go. Yellow taxis like this one are associated with New York City, but they can be found in many cities around the world.

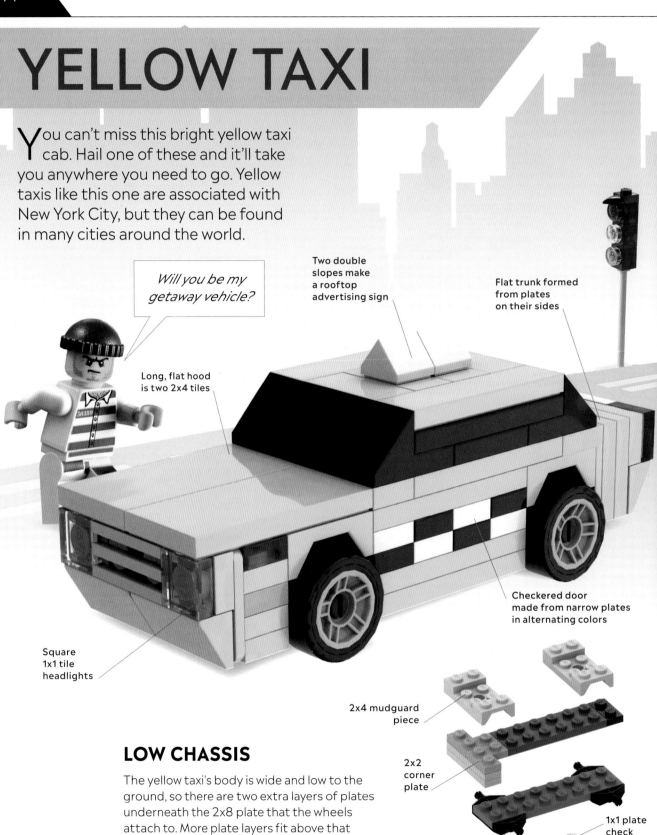

Will you be my getaway vehicle?

Two double slopes make a rooftop advertising sign

Flat trunk formed from plates on their sides

Long, flat hood is two 2x4 tiles

Checkered door made from narrow plates in alternating colors

Square 1x1 tile headlights

2x4 mudguard piece

2x2 corner plate

2x2 plate with wheel-holding pins

1x1 plate check pattern

4x4 plate

LOW CHASSIS

The yellow taxi's body is wide and low to the ground, so there are two extra layers of plates underneath the 2x8 plate that the wheels attach to. More plate layers fit above that plate, including two 2x4 mudguard pieces.

TAXI!

Now the distinctive door pattern is in place. The bottom layer of the checks is made from 1x1 plates, but the top layer is 1x4 plates. The rest of the bodywork is taking shape, too, with front and rear bumpers and head-, tail-, and sidelights.

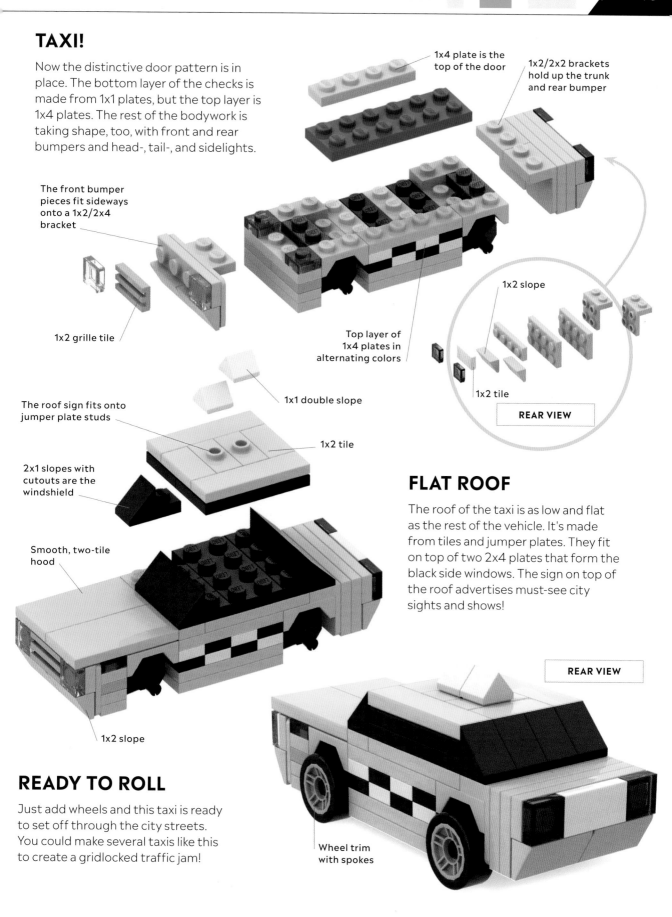

1x4 plate is the top of the door

1x2/2x2 brackets hold up the trunk and rear bumper

The front bumper pieces fit sideways onto a 1x2/2x4 bracket

1x2 grille tile

Top layer of 1x4 plates in alternating colors

1x2 slope

1x2 tile

REAR VIEW

1x1 double slope

The roof sign fits onto jumper plate studs

1x2 tile

2x1 slopes with cutouts are the windshield

Smooth, two-tile hood

FLAT ROOF

The roof of the taxi is as low and flat as the rest of the vehicle. It's made from tiles and jumper plates. They fit on top of two 2x4 plates that form the black side windows. The sign on top of the roof advertises must-see city sights and shows!

1x2 slope

REAR VIEW

READY TO ROLL

Just add wheels and this taxi is ready to set off through the city streets. You could make several taxis like this to create a gridlocked traffic jam!

Wheel trim with spokes

ROAD TRAFFIC CONTROL

There are a lot of objects on or near roads that are there to keep us safe, whether we're in a car or walking or working near them. These road traffic control devices are often overlooked in real life, but they can make a LEGO road more interesting.

TRAFFIC LIGHTS

The red, yellow, and green 1x1 round plate signals on this set of traffic lights slot into the underside of a 2x4 plate.

This is the tube part of a 1x1 round plate

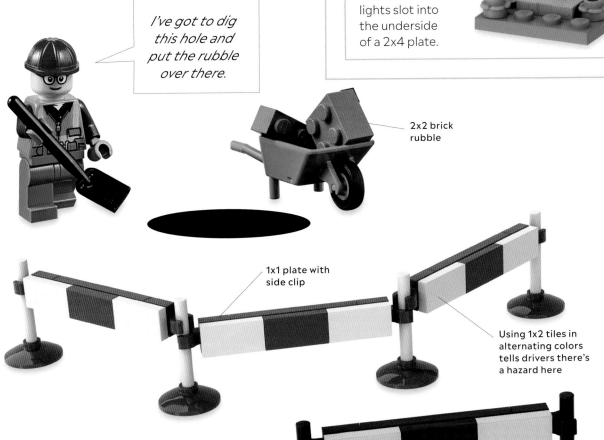

I've got to dig this hole and put the rubble over there.

2x2 brick rubble

1x1 plate with side clip

Using 1x2 tiles in alternating colors tells drivers there's a hazard here

TRAFFIC BARRIERS

Repairing roads (or "roadworks") is a regular—and sometimes annoying—part of everyday life. Try building these traffic barriers to tell your cars to keep away.

Radar dish feet

Sign attaches to a brick with side stud

Pole is a bar piece

TRAFFIC CONES

Make a lot of tiny traffic cones to show your cars where they can and can't go on a road! These build ideas use two different sizes of the LEGO cone piece.

2x2 plate base

1x1 cone

2x2 cone

STOP SIGN

This traffic-stopping road sign is made from a 2x2 round tile with an open stud. A T-piece slots into the stud to make the white "stop" line.

SPEED BUMP

These bumps in the road force cars to slow down on streets where there are a lot of minifigures around. They are easy to make with curved bricks.

I've got to take this rubble and fill up that hole over there.

4x1 double curved slope

There is one 2x8 plate underneath

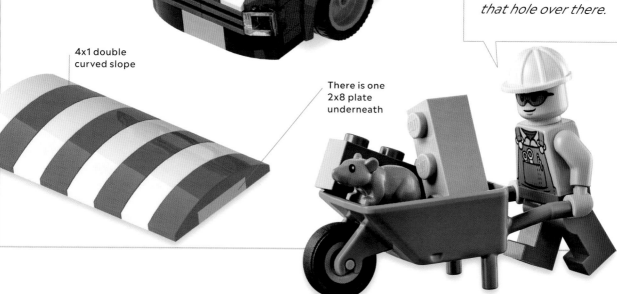

GINGERBREAD CAR

Your minifigures will need a sweet tooth to take a ride in this kooky convertible. It has gingerbread bodywork, seats lined with hard candy, and an ice-cream-emitting exhaust! They'll never need to remember car snacks again.

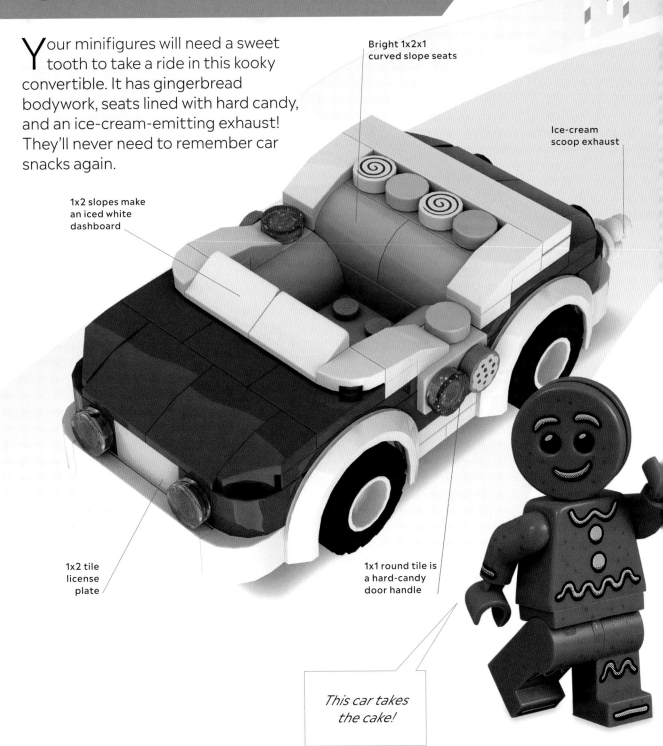

Bright 1x2x1 curved slope seats

Ice-cream scoop exhaust

1x2 slopes make an iced white dashboard

1x2 tile license plate

1x1 round tile is a hard-candy door handle

This car takes the cake!

INGREDIENTS

The base of the gingerbread car is made from bricks and plates in any color, because it can't be seen on the final build. There's a blue 2x10 base plate, with more plates fitted horizontally across it to add width. Bracket pieces at each end hold the front and rear bumper pieces.

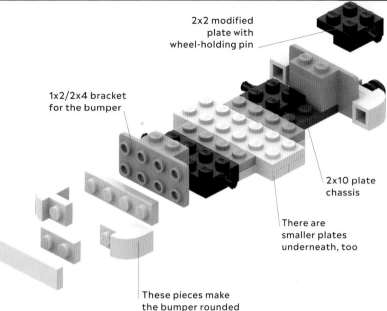

2x2 modified plate with wheel-holding pin

1x2/2x4 bracket for the bumper

2x10 plate chassis

There are smaller plates underneath, too

These pieces make the bumper rounded

SHAPING THE DOUGH

Now the car has round, icing-colored mudguards for the wheels to whirr inside and gingerbread side doors made from inverted slope bricks. The front and back bumpers are in place, too, with headlight and license plate details.

2x1 inverted slope brick

2x2 bricks fill gaps in the middle

Round mudguard piece

Round tile headlight attached to a 1x1 plate

Leave this space for the seats

2x2 curved slope

1x2x1 curved slope armrest

Add a tile on top of this 1x6 plate for a smooth finish

FRESHLY BAKED

Build up the gingerbread hood with brown plates and tiles, then add curved slopes and wedges for a rounded finish. Next, add the wheels and hard-candy details, and this gingerbread car will be ready to serve to your minifigures!

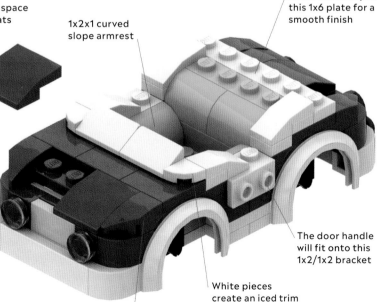

The door handle will fit onto this 1x2/1x2 bracket

White pieces create an iced trim

2x1 wedge on the hood edge

RV

Your minifigures can enjoy the freedom of the open road in this RV! Made for adventure, it's a compact home on wheels, with built-in bunk beds, sitting areas, and a small kitchen. The roof lifts off and one of its sides opens on hinges so it's easy to play inside.

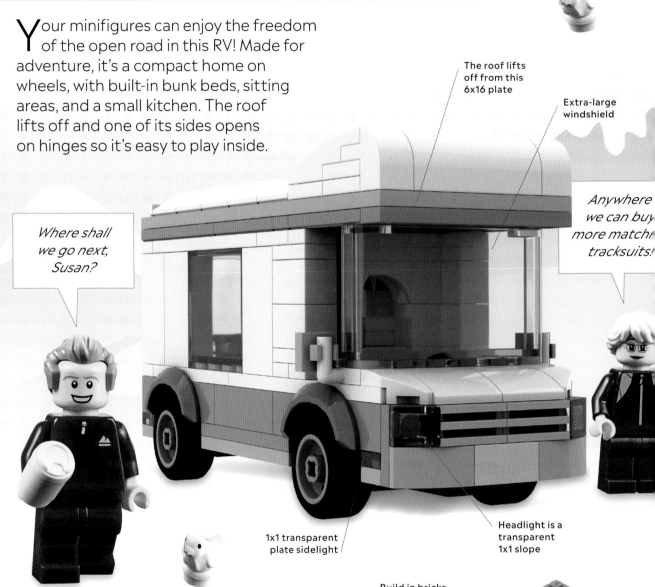

The roof lifts off from this 6x16 plate

Extra-large windshield

Anywhere we can buy more match[ing] tracksuits!

Where shall we go next, Susan?

1x1 transparent plate sidelight

Headlight is a transparent 1x1 slope

HOME SWEET HOME

To build the foundations of this mobile home, start with two 4x8 plates. Attach mudguards above them and wheel-holding plates below, locking them in with another plate underneath. Then build up the sides and bumpers of the RV with more plates and bricks.

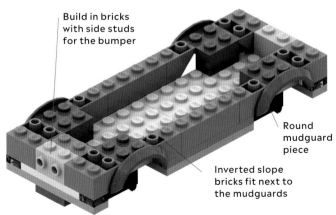

Build in bricks with side studs for the bumper

Round mudguard piece

Inverted slope bricks fit next to the mudguards

KITCHEN EQUIPMENT

Once the hood and front bumper details are in place on the outside of the RV, it's time to think about what your adventuring minifigures might need inside. The kitchen area has everything, including the kitchen sink.

Sink is a 1x2x1 panel with two sides

Jumper plate bench base

Leave room for a driver's seat!

2x2 curved slope hood

1x1 round tile oven hobs

Hinge plates for the opening side door

Side mirror clips onto a vertical bar

Wide window is a 1x3x4 wall element

1x4x1 arch brick

1x6x3 windshield

WINDOWS WITH A VIEW

Build in an extra-wide windshield and windows so your minifigures can take in new landscapes as they drive along! There's now an arched doorway separating the driver's cabin from the living quarters.

4x2 curved slopes

1x2 slopes around the back edges

Stacked-brick side walls

BUNK BEDS

Give your RVers somewhere to rest their head pieces by building bunk beds into the side door of the RV. These ones are made from plates that are partly built into the wall.

Line the top with mostly tiles so the roof can lift off

Susan's coffee on the counter

2x4 tile duvet

1x2 plate with ladder

2x2 tile pillow

REAR VIEW

Small white plates are undersheets!

1x2 brick rear license plate

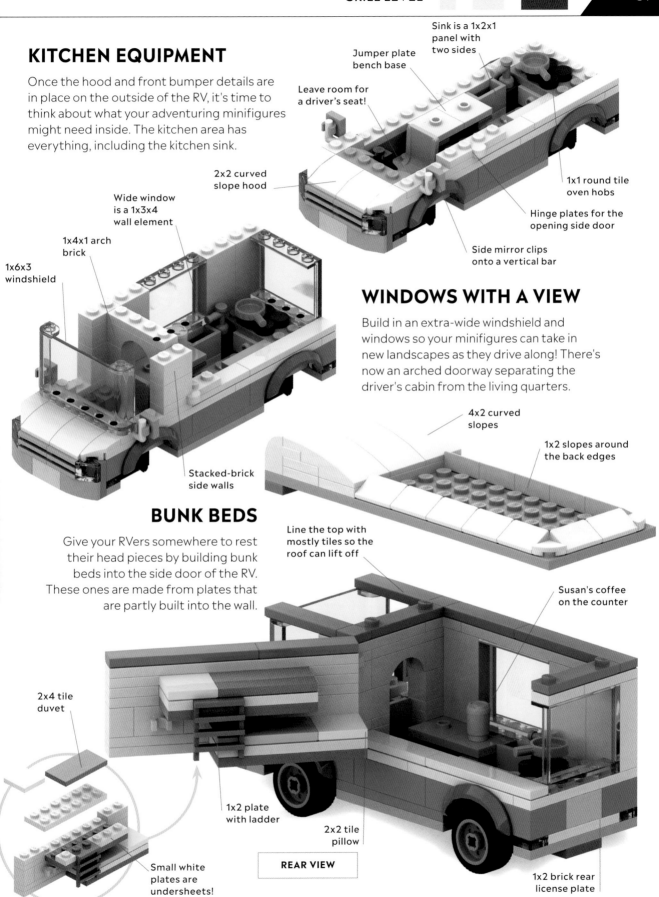

AROUND THE TOWN

There are many familiar roadside sights that your LEGO® cars might whizz past on their road trips. Practical places such as bus stops and newspaper stands, blooming flower planters, and even benches and barriers are all fun to build and play with.

Round plate with flower petals

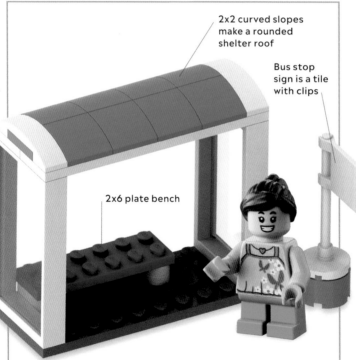

2x2 curved slopes make a rounded shelter roof

Bus stop sign is a tile with clips

2x6 plate bench

1x4 brick with side studs

FLOWER PLANTERS

Bring your LEGO road-users some cheer by building brightly colored flower planters. These planter boxes are built up from 4x6 plates. The tile wooden planks around the edges are attached to bricks with side studs.

BUS STOP

This bus stop has a sturdy sign pole that lets minifigures know which buses stop there. There's also a large shelter with a bench to rest on in case they've just missed one!

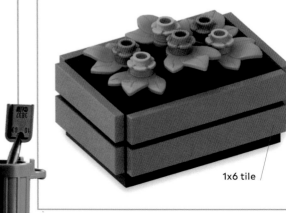

1x6 tile

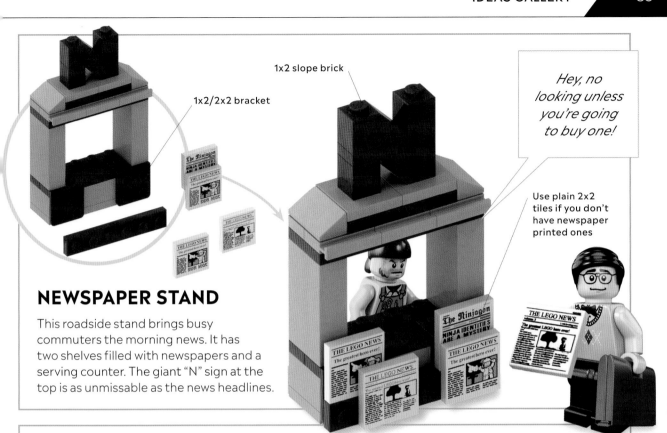

1x2/2x2 bracket

1x2 slope brick

Hey, no looking unless you're going to buy one!

Use plain 2x2 tiles if you don't have newspaper printed ones

NEWSPAPER STAND

This roadside stand brings busy commuters the morning news. It has two shelves filled with newspapers and a serving counter. The giant "N" sign at the top is as unmissable as the news headlines.

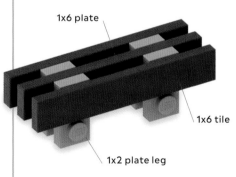

1x6 plate

1x6 tile

1x2 plate leg

1x2 plate in the gap

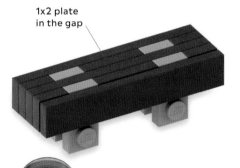

BENCHES

These neat little benches are both built sideways. The first uses long plates and a tile. The second is the same build with smaller plates in the gaps to make the bench solid.

BARRIER

This working barrier prevents cars from going into or out of places. It can raise up thanks to a LEGO Technic pin connection at one end. It also has a ramp underneath to slow cars down when they approach.

LEGO® Technic tile with two pin holes

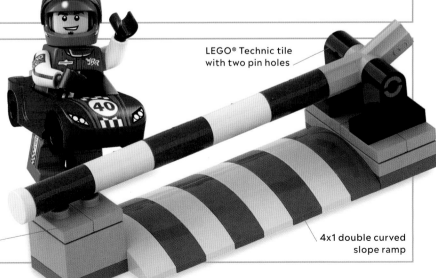

Barrier rests on jumper plates

4x1 double curved slope ramp

ICE-CREAM TRUCK

W hat's that sound? Could it be ...? The ice-cream
truck is here! Hearing the cheerful melodies of
this vehicle brings joy to children and adults alike
on a warm summer day. A quirky and colorful
shop on wheels, the ice-cream truck drives around
residential streets selling
delicious frozen treats
from its serving hatch.

2x2 dome with hole is a scoop of ice cream

A gold 2x2x2 cone makes a tasty-looking waffle cone

Striped roof made from curved slopes and tiles

1x1 half round tiles form the curved ends of this shop sign

I've had a sundae every Sunday since I was a girl.

Bright colors to attract attention from all angles

Vanilla ice cream on the serving counter

WIDE LOAD

The ice-cream truck needs a lot of room inside for freezers and ice-cream-making equipment, so its chassis must be very wide. The bottom layer is actually a narrow 4x12 plate, but more plates on top increase its width. At the front, a brick with side studs allows the bumper parts to attach sideways.

4x6 plate fits into the middle section

5x2x1 bracket

Modified 1x2 brick has four side studs

2x2 plate

Modified 2x6 plate

Two 1x2 grille tiles form one engine grille

2x1 curved slope bumper

These pieces can be any color

Tap piece is the vanilla nozzle

Handle made from a round plate with bar

1x2 plate with pin hole holds the headlight

2x2 curved slope hood

1x2 grille tile drainer

ICE-CREAM MACHINE

After building up the lower sides of the truck, create some of the inside details, such as a chocolate and vanilla soft-serve ice-cream machine and popsicles on a counter. Leave space for a driver's seat, too.

Modified 1x4 tile with two studs

2x6x2 windshield

REMOVABLE ROOF

The ice-cream truck needs an extra-wide windshield for spotting hungry customers and a large serving counter for handing over its wares. The last part of the build is the striped roof, which can easily be lifted off the six studs at the top of the van.

Three plates for the counter

ROYAL CAR

This car can really stop traffic—and for good reason! It's built to carry LEGO royalty and other VIPs to their very important appointments. A shiny gold crown sits atop its classy black bodywork, and there's even a red carpet inside for the minifigure monarch.

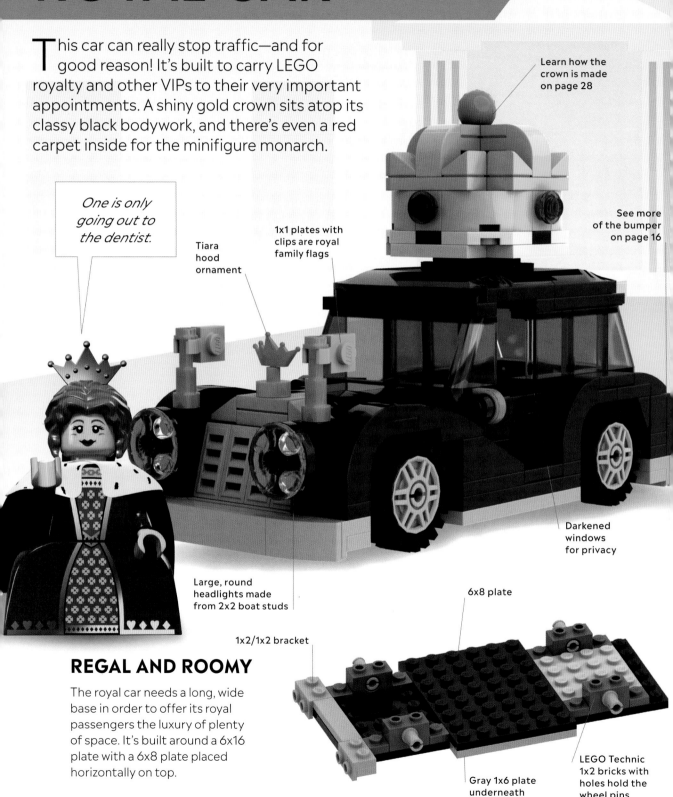

One is only going out to the dentist.

Learn how the crown is made on page 28

Tiara hood ornament

1x1 plates with clips are royal family flags

See more of the bumper on page 16

Darkened windows for privacy

Large, round headlights made from 2x2 boat studs

6x8 plate

1x2/1x2 bracket

REGAL AND ROOMY

The royal car needs a long, wide base in order to offer its royal passengers the luxury of plenty of space. It's built around a 6x16 plate with a 6x8 plate placed horizontally on top.

Gray 1x6 plate underneath

LEGO Technic 1x2 bricks with holes hold the wheel pins

CROWN CURVES

The royal car now has its seats and red carpet on the inside. Its shiny curved sides and silver trim on the outside make it stand out as a top-quality car.

4x1 curved slope

1x3x2 arch brick

Comfortable rear seat

1x2 tile armrests

Four slotted slopes form the front grille

T-piece holds the wheel

Build up the hood with bricks and plates

Tile red carpet wraps around the driver's seat

STEER CLEAR

Instead of a steering wheel panel, the royal car has steering built into a dashboard made from a bracket and two plates with clips.

The headlights will attach here

This plate with ring is the base of the side mirror

The windows are topped with mostly tiles so the roof can lift off

1x2x2 panel window

ROYAL PROTECTION

Now the royal car has a sloping, smooth hood made from curved slopes to protect its engine. It also has a smoked glass windshield and windows to protect its passengers' privacy.

The hood ornament fits onto this stud

1x1 round tile with bar

2x2 plates and boat studs make curved headlights

AROUND THE RACETRACK

A racetrack is more than a circuit for your speediest LEGO cars to race around. Creating some of these little models will turn a road into a lively racing arena. Ready ... set ... RACE!

The top racer wins this trophy

You could also make square platforms with plates

Each number is made from smaller plates in a contrasting color

PODIUM

This is where all racing drivers want to be at the end of a race! The three platforms of this podium are made from plates and curved slope bricks.

Flagpoles attach to 1x4 plates with two studs

Bricks in different sizes form the stepped sides

One 2x8 plate bench can hold several minifigures

1x2 brick

2x8 plates form the barrier's base

1x8 tile

2x2 slope brick

GRANDSTAND

Speed-loving spectators can sit together on this grandstand and watch the action whizz by on the track. Each stepped layer of seats is made from two 2x8 plates, which rest on three sections of bricks.

CRASH BARRIER

Racing cars move at huge speeds and they can sometimes crash. These protective barriers stop spectators from getting hurt. They are made from regular and sloped bricks, with tiles on top.

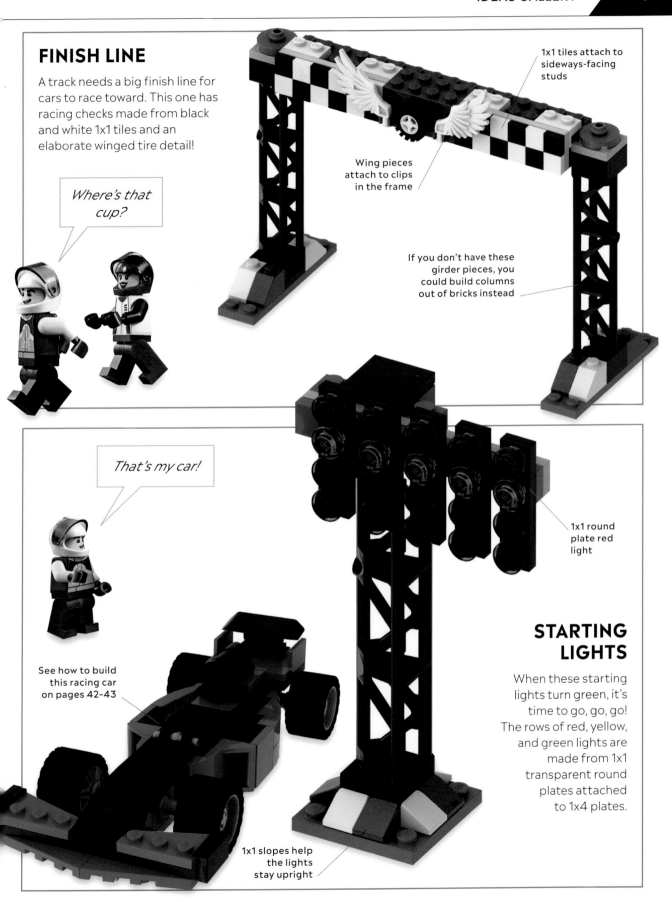

FINISH LINE

A track needs a big finish line for cars to race toward. This one has racing checks made from black and white 1x1 tiles and an elaborate winged tire detail!

1x1 tiles attach to sideways-facing studs

Wing pieces attach to clips in the frame

If you don't have these girder pieces, you could build columns out of bricks instead

Where's that cup?

That's my car!

See how to build this racing car on pages 42-43

STARTING LIGHTS

When these starting lights turn green, it's time to go, go, go! The rows of red, yellow, and green lights are made from 1x1 transparent round plates attached to 1x4 plates.

1x1 round plate red light

1x1 slopes help the lights stay upright

MONSTER TRUCK

Smaller automobiles cower at the sight of this beast of a car—it can crush them in seconds! A monster truck is a regular pick-up truck or car that has been modified to have enormous wheels and intimidating features, such as an exposed engine, bright lights, bumper bars, and even chomping teeth.

Floodlights are the undersides of 1x1 round plates

2x2x3 slope bricks support the roof

A monster truck this terrifying is a rare sight.

Bumper bars made from prison window bars

These tires are often seen on LEGO tractors

Tooth plates hang from the bumper

4x3x1 curved mudguard

1x14 LEGO Technic brick with holes

5x2x1 brack[e]

2x2 brick with pins and axle h[o]

MONSTROUS BASE

This is a chassis built around two LEGO Technic bricks with holes, which attach to three 4x4 plates below. Wide, arched mudguard pieces fit onto the bricks. Bricks with pin holes and large bracket pieces sit inside the space between the longer bricks with holes.

Enormous wheels hang from these two pins

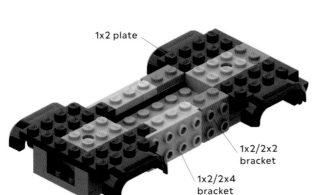

1x2 plate

1x2/2x2 bracket

1x2/2x4 bracket

BEFORE THE BODYWORK

Add plates in different sizes on top of the chassis base, along with pieces with side studs on the outer edges. The smoother bodywork pieces will then attach to those side studs in the next stages of the build.

Find more bumper builds on pages 16–17

2x2 driver's seat

1x2/2x2 bracket

TERRIFYING TEETH

Monsters have sharp teeth, so monster trucks should have them, too! These teeth are attached before the truck's front bumper details are. They fit onto bracket pieces with sideways studs.

1x2 plate with three teeth

1x1 plate with one horizontal tooth

This 2x2 curved slope is part of the side door

HUGE ENGINE

If the monster truck's teeth aren't enough to scare passing motorists, its exposed engine might be! Its made from plates with angled tubes and a large "air-scoop" piece, which supplies air to the engine.

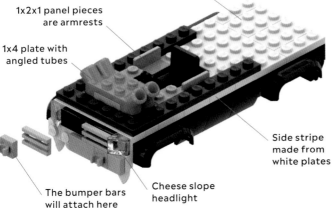

These plates are the cargo area

1x2x1 panel pieces are armrests

1x4 plate with angled tubes

Side stripe made from white plates

The bumper bars will attach here

Cheese slope headlight

4x6 plate roof

The sides of the cargo area are panel pieces

3x6x2 windshield

Bumper bars are a 1x4x3 bar with grille piece

ENCLOSED CABIN

The daring minifigure driver of the monster truck needs the protection of a strong roof, so cover the driver's cabin with a 4x6 plate. Finally, attach LEGO Technic liftarm pieces below the mudguards— these will hold the thundering wheels.

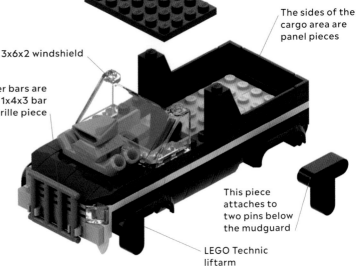

This piece attaches to two pins below the mudguard

LEGO Technic liftarm

IN THE GARAGE

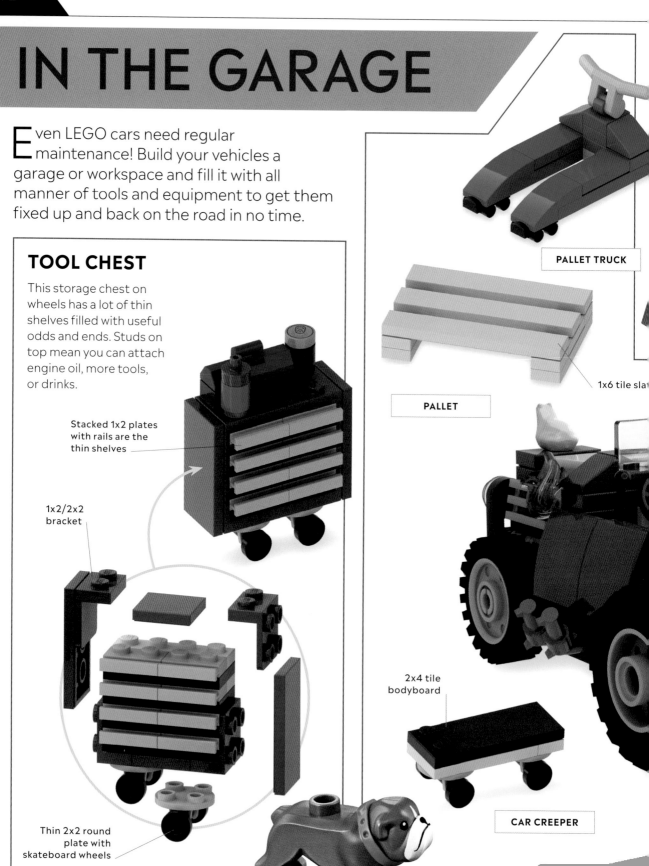

Even LEGO cars need regular maintenance! Build your vehicles a garage or workspace and fill it with all manner of tools and equipment to get them fixed up and back on the road in no time.

TOOL CHEST

This storage chest on wheels has a lot of thin shelves filled with useful odds and ends. Studs on top mean you can attach engine oil, more tools, or drinks.

Stacked 1x2 plates with rails are the thin shelves

1x2/2x2 bracket

Thin 2x2 round plate with skateboard wheels

PALLET TRUCK

PALLET

1x6 tile slat

2x4 tile bodyboard

CAR CREEPER

WORK BENCH

This well-equipped work bench has a tough surface for sawing, hammering, and drilling. It has lots of clips for hanging tools to and a vice for gripping things.

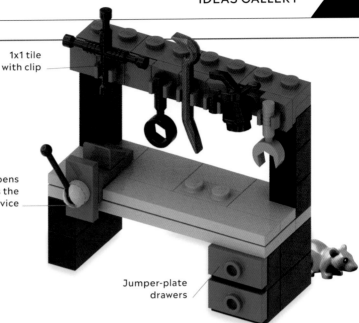

1x1 tile with clip

Lever opens and closes the jaws of the vice

Dont forget the most important thing— a coffeepot!

Jumper-plate drawers

TINY TOOLS

Think of all the things you might see in a mechanic's workplace. Here are some ideas for smaller mechanical tools and equipment for fixing vehicles.

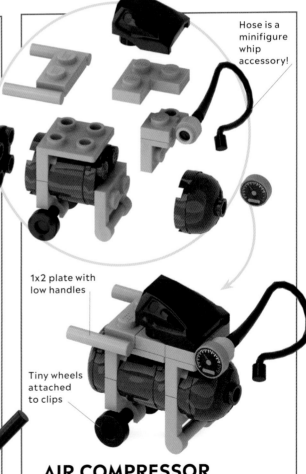

Hose is a minifigure whip accessory!

1x2 plate with low handles

Tiny wheels attached to clips

See how to build this hot rod on pages 68-69

This 1x2 plate with bar handle moves on a clip

TROLLEY JACK

AIR COMPRESSOR

This tool has a tank filled with tightly compressed air. Its hose attaches to cars' tires and pumps them up.

LIMOUSINE

This chauffeur-driven stretch limousine is a party on wheels! Its luxurious interior has a swanky sofa, its own karaoke machine, and best of all a hot tub at the rear. Just don't make any sharp turns!

This is great if you ignore the honking!

6x2x3 windshield

Three 2x4 tiles create a sharp-edged hood

Small curved slopes form the rounded bumper

Opening side door has two hinge-plate connections

Transparent blue 1x2 plates and tiles are whirling hot-tub water

STRETCHED CHASSIS

An extra-long car needs a double-length chassis. The limousine's base is made from two ready-made chassis pieces. There are two plates with wheel pins at either end of the chassis and white plates underneath and around them.

2x2 modified plate with wheel-holding pin

4x10 chassis piece with recessed center

2x4 plate

The rear bumper will attach to these modified plates with side studs

2x2 corner plate

CHAUFFEUR'S SEAT

After building up the chassis with plates, add crisp white mudguards above the wheel-holding pins and put in a seat and steering wheel for the chauffeur. At the back, add bricks and more plates to create a raised section for the hot tub.

These small plates won't be seen in the final model so they can be any color

4x2 mudguard with arch

Dual headlights made from a 1x2 rounded plate and two 1x1 round tiles

1x1 plate with ring side mirror

1x4 brick with side studs

Combining four 2x1 slopes with slots makes a pointed grille

The door fits onto this swiveling hinge-plate connection

BUMPER TO BUMPER

Both the limousine's bumpers are built separately from the main build. The front bumper has a pointed silver grille and dual headlights for a glitzy look. There are matching dual taillights on the rear bumper that are made using the same technique.

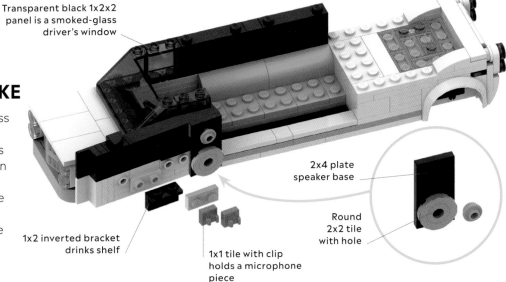

Transparent black 1x2x2 panel is a smoked-glass driver's window

CAR KARAOKE

Add the smoked-glass windshield and blacked-out windows of the limousine, then get ready to party! Build pieces with side studs into the door to attach the karaoke sound system and other fun details to.

1x2 inverted bracket drinks shelf

1x1 tile with clip holds a microphone piece

2x4 plate speaker base

Round 2x2 tile with hole

RAISING THE ROOF

The long white roof has a base layer of plates topped with tiles and curved slopes. It attaches to four exposed studs on one side of the limousine so it can be removed easily.

These plates fill a gap between the door and the roof

Modified 1x4 plate with two studs

This tile at the top of the door helps you open it

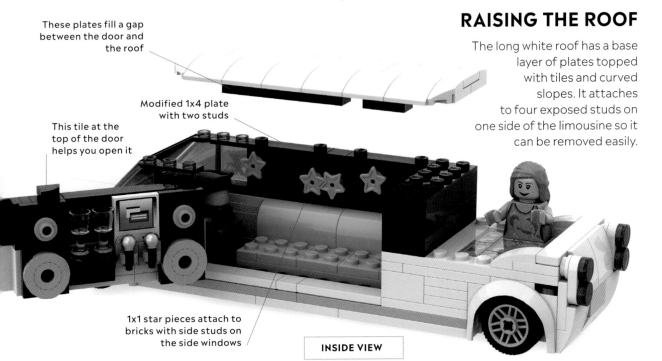

1x1 star pieces attach to bricks with side studs on the side windows

INSIDE VIEW

Penguin
Random
House

Senior Editor **Helen Murray**
Project Art Editor **Jenny Edwards**
Senior Production Editor **Jennifer Murray**
Senior Production Controller **Louise Minihane**
Managing Editor **Paula Regan**
Managing Art Editor **Jo Connor**
Publishing Director **Mark Searle**

Packaged for DK by **Plum Jam**
Editor **Hannah Dolan** Designer **Guy Harvey**

Models designed and created by **Nate Dias**

Dorling Kindersley would like to thank: **Randi Sørensen**,
Heidi K. Jensen, **Paul Hansford**, **Martin Leighton**
Lindhardt, **Nina Koopmann**, **Charlotte Neidhardt**,
and **Lis Christensen** at the LEGO Group; **Nate Dias** for
supplying all model images and breakdowns; **Jessica**
Farrell for LEGO building insights; and **Julia March**
and **Jennette ElNaggar** at DK for proofreading.

First American Edition, 2021
Published in the United States by DK Publishing
1745 Broadway, 20th Floor, New York NY 10019

Page design copyright © 2021 Dorling Kindersley Limited
DK, a Division of Penguin Random House LLC
23 24 25 10 9 8 7 6 5 4
011–324047–Oct/2021

Manufactured by Dorling Kindersley, One Embassy Gardens,
8 Viaduct Gardens, London SW11 7BW, under license from
the LEGO Group.

A catalog record for this book
is available from the Library of Congress.
ISBN 978-0-7440-3968-9

DK books are available at special discounts when purchased
in bulk for sales promotions, premiums, fund-raising,
or educational use.
For details, contact: DK Publishing Special Markets,
1745 Broadway, 20th Floor, New York NY 10019
SpecialSales@dk.com

Printed and bound in China

www.dk.com/legocars

www.LEGO.com

MIX
Paper | Supporting
responsible forestry
FSC™ C018179

This book was made with
Forest Stewardship Council™
certified paper—one small
step in DK's commitment
to a sustainable future.